To the Rescue!

The SeaWorld/Busch Gardens Animal Rescue and Rehabilitation Program

To the Rescue!
The SeaWorld/Busch Gardens
Animal Rescue and Rehabilitation Program

PART OF THE SEAWORLD EDUCATION SERIES

Research/Writing/Layout
Donna Parham

Technical Advisors
Brad Andrews
Laura Collins
Tom Goff
Raina Grable
John Kerivan
Jim McBain, D.V.M.
Daniel K. Odell, Ph.D.
Jack Pearson
Tom Reidarson, D.V.M.
Kevin Robinson
Mike Shaw
Bea Stark
Wendy Turner
Gary Violetta
Jody Westberg
Dudley Wigdahl
Laura Wittish
Keith Yip
Pamela Yochem, D.V.M.
Glenn Young

Education Directors
Lorna Crane
Hollis Gillespie
Bob Mindick
Joy L. Wolf

Editorial Staff
Jody Byrum
Deborah Nuzzolo
Donna Parham
Judith Swift
Loran Wlodarski

Photos
Mike Aguilera
Bob Couey
Bob French
Chris Gotshall
Guy Nickerson, Spectrum Productions
Norma Roberts
Judy St. Leger, D.V.M.
Melinda Tucker
Jim Tuten
Mike Wallace
SeaWorld and Busch Gardens
   Photo Departments

ISBN 1-893698-06-8

©2001 Sea World, Inc. All Rights Reserved.

Published by SeaWorld San Diego
500 SeaWorld Drive, San Diego, California, 92109-7904

CONTENTS

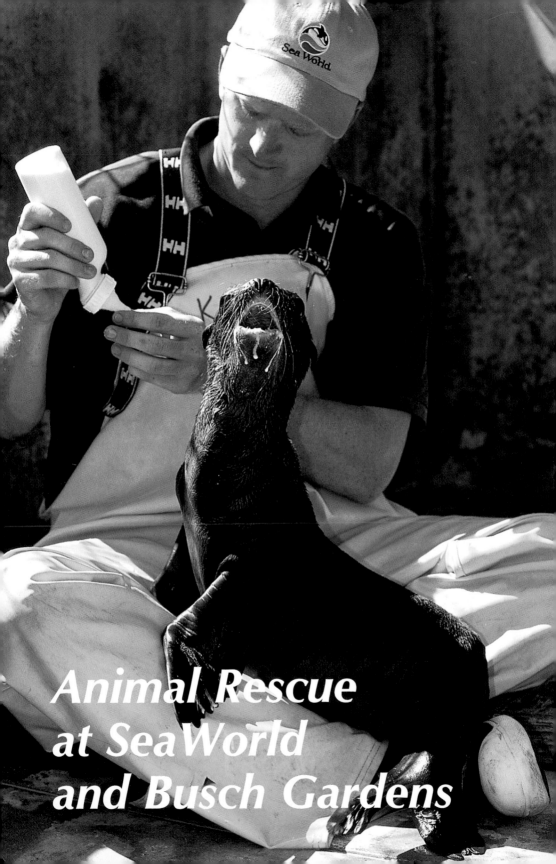

Animal Rescue
at SeaWorld
and Busch Gardens

The SeaWorld/Busch Gardens Animal Rescue and Rehabilitation Program is an important part of SeaWorld and Busch Gardens  Adventure Parks' commitment to conservation, research, and education. Through this program, SeaWorld and Busch Gardens devote around-the-clock and across-the-globe resources and technology to rescue, treat, shelter, and release thousands of stranded, sick, and injured animals.

The main objective of the SeaWorld/Busch Gardens Animal Rescue and Rehabilitation Program is to return rehabilitated animals to the wild. Perhaps as important, the program affords wildlife experts the opportunity to learn—in an intimate, hands-on way—about the kinds of environmental problems that impact wild animals. Rescued animals provide insights into their species' biology and ecology, and the information gathered from wildlife rescues is a valuable source of knowledge that can be used in making wildlife management decisions.

All four SeaWorld parks—SeaWorld San Diego, SeaWorld Cleveland, SeaWorld San Antonio, and SeaWorld Orlando—participate in the program, as does Busch Gardens Tampa Bay, another Anheuser-Busch Adventure Park. Since the program began in 1965, SeaWorld and Busch Gardens have rescued more than 12,000 animals representing more than 140 species of whales, dolphins, manatees, otters, pinnipeds, turtles, and birds. The ability to rescue and rehabilitate stranded animals is the result of years of experience caring for animals at the parks.

SeaWorld and Busch Gardens parks cover virtually all expenses of the SeaWorld/Busch Gardens Animal Rescue and Rehabilitation Program, including staff, transportation, and facilities, at an annual cost well over $1 million.

Chapter One

Why Do Animals Strand?

"**What befalls the earth befalls the sons of the earth.**"

Seattle, patriarch of the Duwamish and Squamish Indians of Puget Sound

A California sea lion (*Zalophus californianus*) strands on the beach.

What's wrong with that animal?

Have you ever seen a marine mammal on the beach? A whale or dolphin on the beach is in obvious need of help, but healthy seals, sea lions, walruses, and otters naturally haul out onto land at times. They may haul out to mate or to bear their young. Some haul out while molting (shedding old fur and growing a new coat of fur). And sometimes they haul out simply to rest.

It can be hard to tell if an animal on the beach is a stranded animal in need of help, or a healthy animal showing natural behavior. Imagine you encounter a small sea lion pup on the beach. Thin and feeble, it cries plaintively. Is it in need of help? Maybe not. It may be a healthy newborn—its mother foraging nearby.

But sometimes, an animal hauls out because it is ill, injured, or weak. In this case, an animal is considered stranded. The term *stranded* refers to a live marine animal that is helpless and unable to cope in its present position. The term generally is used to refer to marine mammals or sea turtles. SeaWorld and Busch Gardens also rescue a variety of ill and injured birds, and in this book, the term *stranded* refers to distressed birds as well. Examples of stranded animals include a dolphin lying on the beach, a seal that is out of its range, a pelican blown off course, or an icebound whale.

The terms *stranded* and *beached* can, for the most part, be used interchangeably, but *beached* often refers to dead animals on the beach, while *stranded* usually refers to live animals.

A marine animal may strand if it is affected by a severe, debilitating illness or injury, or if it is too weak to swim or hunt for food. To avoid predators, a wild animal with an illness or injury generally tries to mask its symptoms for as long as possible. When birds, marine mammals, or sea turtles strand, death is usually imminent if there is no intervention.

The following pages in this chapter describe some of the most common reasons for stranding.

Under the streets of Vero Beach, two Florida manatees *(Trichechus manatus latirostris)* swam a half mile up this storm drain pipe before they got stuck in shallow water. Here a SeaWorld animal rescue expert surveys the situation in preparation for rescuing the manatees.

Diseases

Marine animals are susceptible to a variety of viral, bacterial, and fungal infections. Marine mammals may develop stomach ulcers, skin diseases, hepatitis, cancer, tuberculosis, and respiratory disorders such as pneumonia.

Hundreds of marine mammals have stranded following outbreaks of morbillivirus. Morbilliviruses are a group of viruses that include human measles and canine distemper. Related morbilliviruses have caused massive outbreaks—and strandings—in some seal and dolphin populations in the Atlantic Ocean, the Mediterranean Sea, and the Gulf of Mexico. In the late 1990s, 18 common dolphins (*Delphinus* spp.) stranded on the California coast. Lab results from six of the dolphins revealed the first morbilliviral infections seen in free-ranging cetaceans off the Pacific coast of North America.

Diseases of waterfowl and seabirds vary with habitat and food preferences. Infectious diseases may spread through entire waterfowl and seabird populations, resulting in mass die-offs. Migrating waterfowl spread disease further. Infections include viral hepatitis, Newcastle disease, tuberculosis, tetanus, duck plague (duck virus enteritus), and botulism.

Aspergillosis, a fungal infection transmitted by airborne spores, can affect waterfowl, seabirds, and marine mammals. Aspergillosis infections are likely triggered by lowered resistance or environmental factors.

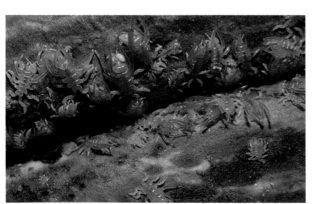

These whale lice (*Cyamus* spp.) are natural parasites that live on whales, feeding on a whale's skin. On injured whales, they also feed on the damaged tissue of wounds.

California sea lions like this one are hosts for the roundworm *Parafilaroides decorus,* also called lungworm. Lungworms live in the sea lion's lung tissue or airways, where they can make breathing difficult. A lungworm infestation develops gradually and is well established before it becomes apparent.

Parasites

Parasites may infest the skin, digestive tract, heart, brain, and other organs of birds, marine mammals, and sea turtles. In most cases, parasite infestations alone are unlikely to debilitate otherwise healthy animals, but they may harm animals that are already weakened by other illnesses or injuries. In these cases parasite infestations may make an animal ill and weak, and occasionally result in the animal's death.

Internally, tapeworms, flatworms, and roundworms are common parasites of marine mammals, turtles, and birds. Externally, lice, ticks, and mites live on a bird's skin and feathers. Barnacles may encrust whales, manatees, and sea turtles. Whales can also be infested with a type of crustacean called "whale lice."

Entanglement in marine debris has become an increasing threat to marine animals. Seabirds, marine mammals, sea turtles, fishes, and invertebrates can become trapped or tangled in nets, ropes, fishing line, or other lost or floating fishing gear. Discarded garbage such as plastic bags, sheets, and wrapping bands also entangle marine animals and can make breathing or eating difficult. Without assistance, entanglement can result in injury and death.

Sometimes entangled animals are rescued in the wild, and the rescued animals never need care at SeaWorld's rehabilitation facilities. In 1988, SeaWorld animal rescue experts freed three California gray whales *(Eschrictius robustus)* that had become entangled in drift nets off the coast of San Diego. When rescue experts carefully removed the nets, the whales resumed migration.

SeaWorld animal rescue experts free an entangled California gray whale.

About the size of a match head, a plastic resin pellet is the raw form of plastic after it has been manufactured from petrochemicals. Such pellets are transported in bulk to factories where they are melted and molded into the incredible variety of plastic items that we know and use. Perhaps not surprisingly, some pellets escape into waterways and make their way into the ocean, where they can be eaten by seabirds and other marine animals—which may mistake them for fish eggs or other small prey.

Marine animals that eat jellyfish, such as certain sea turtles, have mistaken plastic bags, plastic sheeting, and balloons for their prey.

Any ingested foreign object can become lodged in an animal's throat or restrict an airway, causing the animal to suffocate or drown. Such objects can obstruct the gastrointestinal tract and cause gastric inflammation, nausea, and loss of appetite that can result in starvation. A fishing hook lodged in the throat or digestive tract can cause discomfort and may make eating difficult. Worse, a hook may puncture an animal's gastrointestinal tract, causing infection that can be fatal. Fish-eating birds and mammals, and manatees grazing on seagrasses, sometimes accidentally swallow fishing hooks.

An ingested fishing hook can cause a tear in the pouch of a pelican (*Pelicanus* spp.). When the pelican catches a fish, the fish slips through the hole before the pelican can swallow it, and the pelican may starve. SeaWorld San Diego bird experts treat numerous pelicans with pouch tears.

A pelican's bill has a flexible pouch—an adaptation for catching and holding fish.

Titus the Tangled Manatee

On August 8, 1998, SeaWorld Orlando animal care specialists responded to a stranded animal alert. A female manatee was stranded near Titusville, Florida.

Fishing line severely entangled the manatee's right and left flippers. Worse, a large portion of her left flipper was so damaged by the lack of blood circulation to the extremity that more than half of it spontaneously amputated during the rescue.

When SeaWorld Orlando's manatee rescue team was able to do a close inspection of the animal after the rescue, they feared the manatee might become a double-amputee. They quickly and carefully transported the animal in the specially equipped animal rescue unit to SeaWorld Orlando to begin critical emergency treatment.

SeaWorld veterinarians were able to save the manatee's right flipper, and animal care specialists nursed the injured manatee back to health. She was named "Titus," after Titusville, the area in which she was spotted in distress.

After a year of rehabilitation at SeaWorld, Titus passed a battery of final examinations and was deemed ready for release.

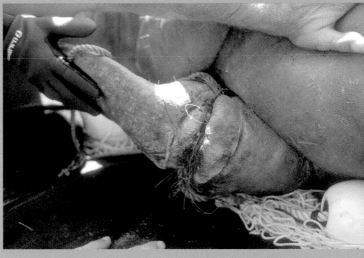

Titus's flippers were so entangled in fishing line that animal care specialists feared she might lose them both. SeaWorld veterinarians were able to save her right flipper and restore her to good health.

To prepare for her release, Titus was equipped with a tiny PIT tag, which will allow wildlife experts to identify her in the future. (See page 77 for more information about PIT tags.)

A boat propeller severely damaged this young manatee's paddle (tail). Despite concentrated efforts to treat the massive wounds, the paddle ultimately had to be amputated by veterinarians in order to save the animal's life.

Traumatic injuries

Like all wild animals, marine animals can become injured in a variety of ways. In addition to the direct harm traumatic injuries cause, untreated wounds are prone to bacterial infections.

Some injuries are the result of the hazards of the natural environment. Fierce battles over territorial disputes during the mating season result in injuries to some male seals, sea lions, and walruses. And a marine mammal that survives attack from a predator such as a shark or killer whale is likely to come away with injuries ranging from mere scrapes to life-threatening gashes.

Seabirds are sometimes injured during storms. Gusty winds can toss chicks from their nests, and strong winds and waves may thrash birds along rocky shorelines, sometimes resulting in concussions or fractured limbs.

Tragically, other injuries are related to human interaction. Motor boats and other watercraft cause substantial wounds to manatees, sea turtles, and dolphins. Birds are sometimes hit by cars. And in spite of the many regulations to protect them, marine mammals are occasionally found with gunshot wounds, especially in areas where there are conflicts over food between the mammals and fishermen. Similarly, some sea turtles and pelicans have been found with head injuries that suggest blows to the head with blunt or sharp objects.

Stranding at low tide

In areas where the tidal change is significant, marine animals may be caught unaware when the tide recedes. For example, beluga whales *(Delphinapterus leucas)* sometimes become stranded in tide pools at low tide. They generally survive until the next high tide and swim away unharmed.

Rarely, whales or dolphins are left "high and dry" at low tide. Unless they are carried back to the water, they may not survive.

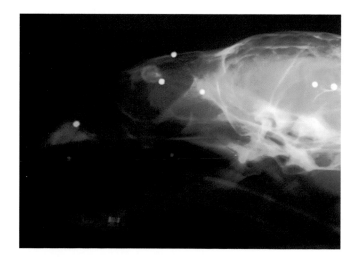

This head x-ray of a rescued California sea lion revealed buckshot lodged in the head. In spite of regulations to protect marine mammals, they are sometimes found with wounds caused by people.

The natural homes of plants and animals can be destroyed in the course of development and natural resources harvesting. When a habitat is destroyed, some of the animals forced out may not be able to relocate or adapt to a new environment.

One species that faces extensive habitat loss is the endangered Attwater's prairie chicken *(Tympanuchus cupido attwateri)*. Historically, a million Attwater's prairie chickens once inhabited coastal grasslands in Louisiana and Texas, but agriculture, urban and industrial expansion, and overgrazing by cattle all contributed to habitat loss, and by 1996 the Attwater's prairie chicken population had plummeted alarmingly to just 42 birds.

Today, there is a recovery plan for Attwater's prairie chicken, and SeaWorld San Antonio is helping. Rescue efforts for this species consist of captive breeding programs, research, and special care. The ultimate goal is to reintroduce 5,000 captive-bred birds into secure habitat. Integral to the recovery program is the Attwater's prairie chicken Species Survival Plan, administered by the American Zoo and Aquarium Association (AZA). (See pages 84–87 for more information about Species Survival Plans.)

SeaWorld San Antonio participates in a breeding program for Attwater's prairie chicken, a species threatened by habitat destruction.

When a large iron-ore carrier sank off the west coast of South Africa, oil gushed into the sea, and thousands of African penguins *(Spheniscus demersus)* were fouled with oil. Rescuers transported the oiled penguins to Cape Town in cardboard boxes for rehabilitation. SeaWorld bird experts flew in to help rescue and rehabilitate the penguins, a threatened species.

Oil spills

Oil production and transportation pose a threat to marine life. Fouled with oil, sea otters and seabirds lose the insulative qualities of their fur or feathers and are susceptible to hypothermia. They are also likely to ingest the toxic crude oil. Other marine animals are affected, too, when their habitat is destroyed. The California Oiled Wildlife Care Network, supported by industry and government, provides emergency care to oiled wildlife and ensures that marine mammals, birds, and the petroleum industry can share coastal waterways. (See pages 46–47 for more information about SeaWorld San Diego's role in the California Oiled Wildlife Care Network.)

Stranded Far From Home

In July 1990, SeaWorld's stranded animal recovery team responded to a report of a seal in distress on San Diego's Silver Strand Beach. When they arrived on the scene, they were astonished to find a female hooded seal—the first-ever sighting of a hooded seal in the Pacific Ocean. Normally found along the coasts of Newfoundland, Greenland, and Iceland, the seal was more than 12,800 km (8,000 mi.) outside her range.

Marine mammals, turtles, and birds sometimes strand far from where they usually live. In December 1999 a Kemp's ridley sea turtle christened "Beaky" was found stranded on the shores of the Wales Sealife Aquarium in the United Kingdom—some 8,045 km (5,000 mi.) from its native waters of the Gulf of Mexico. The wayward turtle was flown to SeaWorld Orlando for rehabilitation and release into Gulf waters.

Birds are sometimes blown off course by storms. SeaWorld and Busch Gardens parks have rescued and rehabilitated out-of-range birds including sooty shearwaters (*Puffinus griseus*) and Laysan albatross (*Diomedea immutabilis*) in San Diego.

Upon arrival at Orlando, Florida, "Beaky," a Kemp's ridley sea turtle, is examined by a SeaWorld veterinarian.

Toxins

Both natural toxins and human-made toxins can harm or kill animals. Some substances (which may not be harmful in small quantities) are stored in an animal's body tissues after they are ingested. Prey animals that contain such toxins in their bodies pass the toxins on to animals higher in the food chain. Predatory fishes, marine mammals, and seabirds may accumulate high levels of natural or human-made toxins. Some toxins can be accumulated by fish and invertebrates without ill effects, but cause poisoning when those "toxic" animals are ingested by mammals or birds.

Some natural toxins originate in certain species of phyto-plankton (tiny floating or drifting algae). Occasionally, phytoplankton reproduce quickly in explosive seasonal population increases called blooms. Some phytoplankton contain reddish pigments, and a bloom may color the water red or rust-colored. Such a bloom is sometimes called a "red tide." In sufficient quantities, some phytoplankton toxins are harmful — even deadly — to mammals and birds.

Ciguatoxin is a natural toxin that originates in certain tropical phytoplankton. *(Gambierdiscus toxicus* is the phytoplankton most noted for production of ciguatoxin, although certain other phytoplankton species also produce it.) Foraging her-bivorous reef fishes ingest the phytoplankton, accumulating ciguatoxin in their tissues. Toxic fishes are eaten by predatory fishes, marine mammals, and seabirds. The concentration of ciguatoxin can reach deadly levels in the tissues of large predators, including humans. The resulting condition is known as ciguatera poisoning.

In 1996 and 1997, more than 160 Florida manatee deaths were attributed to brevitoxin poisoning. Like ciguatoxin, brevitoxin is produced by a species of phytoplankton *(Ptychodiscus brevis).* When scientists examined the dead manatees, they found brevitoxin in the stomach contents and lung tissues, suggesting that the manatees ingested the deadly phytoplankton and also inhaled the toxic fumes these phytoplankton produce.

The deaths of more than 400 California sea lions in 1998 and more than 100 brown pelicans *(P. occidentalis)* and cormorants *(Phalacrocorax* spp.) in 1991 all were traced to another phytoplankton (several species of *Pseudonitzschia)*, which produces toxic domoic acid. The affected seabirds and sea lions had been feeding on anchovies that were reported to be feeding on a very intense bloom of the toxic phytoplankton.

The bacteria *Clostridium botulinum* produces a toxin responsible for botulism, a type of food poisoning. SeaWorld bird rehabilitation experts have assisted with the medical care and rehabilitation of pelicans suffering from suspected botulism poisoning.

Human-made toxins also can be found in the marine ecosystem. Industrial and agricultural compounds flow into waterways, eventually making their way to the oceans. Some of these toxins, such as metals and certain fat-soluble compounds, enter the food chain in the same way as natural toxins. In sufficient quantities, some of these substances may harm marine animals.

Scientists are studying the effects of some of these contaminants to see how they affect marine mammals. The PCBs (polychlorinated biphenyls) are one type of environmental contaminant. Scientists found that high concentrations of PCBs lowered reproductive success in certain laboratory animals, but a wide variance in sensitivity among mammals makes generalization to marine mammals difficult. Another hypothesis is that chronic exposure to PCBs or similar compounds can suppress a marine mammal's immune system and make it more susceptible to disease. Research is ongoing.

Adapted for life in warm waters, manatees are likely to succumb to extremely or unseasonably cold weather. Very cold water can also present problems for sea turtles, which are cold-blooded reptiles with metabolism dependent on environmental temperature.

The warm waters of an El Niño event present different problems for marine animals. El Niño is a complex set of cyclic atmospheric changes, characterized by an unusually warm water current in the Eastern Pacific Ocean. As water temperature changes, plankton and fish populations shift, and marine mammals may find their food sources in decline.

Increased storm activity is yet another effect of an El Niño. Storms and other bad weather can make swimming, feeding, and keeping warm difficult, especially for a young marine mammal. Unable to feed, it loses blubber and becomes thin. When it finally strands, an animal is exhausted and emaciated.

SeaWorld San Diego rescues and cares for dozens of stranded elephant seal *(Mirounga angustirostris)* **pups during an El Niño event.**

This Guadalupe fur seal *(Arctocephalus townsendi)* stranded on a San Diego beach underweight, exhausted, and emaciated. Guadalupe fur seals are an endangered species.

Separation

During storms or in times of danger, a young animal may become separated from its mother before it is weaned (no longer nursing from its mother) and independent. Sometimes mothers die, leaving young behind. An orphaned or separated young animal that had been relying on its mother for food and protection is not likely to survive on its own.

After a seal or sea lion is weaned, the mother and pup of many species separate. Some young seals and sea lions are unable to fend for themselves and don't survive this natural separation process.

Mass strandings

Mass strandings of whales and dolphins are natural phenomena that are largely unexplained. In some cases, herds of healthy whales or dolphins become stranded in shallow areas when the tide goes out, but in most cases the stranded animals are ill.

One theory that has been used to explain mass strandings is that, because many species of dolphins and whales are highly social and tend to stay together, a herd of healthy animals may blindly follow one or two ill animals to shore. Information that marine mammal experts have more recently gathered from mass-stranded animals suggests that this theory is likely flawed.

Medical and handling techniques have been developed to improve the diagnostic approach to mass stranding events, to help clarify the health status of the herd, and to help guide future rescue attempts. More emphasis is being placed on gathering medical data from live as well as dead individuals. When rescuers and stranding experts started analyzing more blood and tissue samples from live animals at mass stranding events, they found that many of these herd members—some outwardly appearing healthy—also were ill.

Blood serum from live, mass-stranded animals also can be banked to allow future testing for diseases and problems that aren't considered at the time of stranding. SeaWorld Orlando's serum bank was a major source of information regarding the history and prevalence of morbillivirus along the Florida coast. The resulting information has yielded several scientific articles regarding this deadly virus in cetaceans.

Over the years, SeaWorld has participated in many rescue efforts for cetaceans involved in mass strandings. Virtually all animals in these mass strandings were ill.

Chapter Two

SeaWorld
To the Rescue

"SeaWorld parks are recognized as leaders and innovators in the field of marine mammal rehabilitation."

Joe Cordaro, Marine Mammal Stranding Network Coordinator, National Marine Fisheries Service, Southwest Region

A t SeaWorld San Diego, animal care specialists Jody Westberg and Kevin Robinson check the stranded animal reporting line. Today, a lifeguard has reported a northern elephant seal pup hauled out on a local beach. The pup may be in need of help.

Before Jody and Kevin leave for the beach, they check the animal rescue vehicle—a four-wheel-drive stakebed truck— to be sure all necessary equipment is loaded. It's all there: a sturdy enclosure for transporting seals and sea lions, two different sizes of hoop nets, a throw net, water sprayers, thick leather safety gloves, latex gloves, net knives, wire snips, and a cellular phone. Kevin and Jody hop in and head for the beach.

Jody explains what all the equipment is for. "We can use the net knives and wire snips to cut away netting if an animal is entangled," she says. She says that sometimes an entangled animal is otherwise healthy, and once the netting or other debris that was wrapped around the animal is removed, the animal eagerly scampers to the water's edge and slips back into the sea.

An elephant seal pup strands on a San Diego beach.

SeaWorld animal rescue experts respond to reported strandings in a four-wheel-drive truck stocked with animal transport enclosures, nets, water sprayers, net knives, and other rescue equipment.

But when an animal needs medical treatment or supportive care, it will be transported to SeaWorld San Diego. Kevin estimates that he has participated in rescuing about 900 marine mammals in the 19 years he has been working at SeaWorld. How do you collect a wild, injured animal? "It depends on the species and on the individual animal," says Kevin. "Sometimes we use a net. If the animal's an infant, sometimes we can just pick it up by hand."

At the beach, Kevin and Jody spot the stranded seal pup, surrounded by a small crowd of onlookers. The pup seems uncomfortable by the attention and proximity of humans, but makes no attempt to flee. Even before they reach the scene, Jody is assessing the situation. "The fact that this animal isn't trying to move away from people is a sign that it's sick," she says. "A healthy elephant seal pup may come ashore to rest, but it will immediately make a dash for the ocean when people approach."

Kevin and Jody discuss their rescue strategy.

A little closer, Jody and Kevin study the pup. Even to a non-expert, it's clear that the animal is skinny — the outline of ribs and pelvic bones show through its skin. Also, its eyes are dry and crusty — a sign of dehydration. (Mucus continually washes over an elephant seal's eyes, giving the eyes of a healthy seal a wet, tear-rimmed appearance.)

Kevin and Jody agree that the animal needs treatment at SeaWorld. They position themselves between the pup and the water and deftly collect the pup using a hoop net. Wearing thick leather gloves, they maneuver the pup into a secure enclosure for its trip to SeaWorld.

A wild animal's fight or flight response is very strong — even in ill animals. "Each circumstance is unique, but you have to anticipate what an animal might do," says Kevin. "If a seal or sea lion gets scared, its natural instinct is to take off for the water. But a sick animal will re-strand — even more exhausted and weak than it was before." An important part of a rescue attempt, says Kevin, is being ready for anything.

Jody takes a few minutes to talk to the onlookers, answering questions about the pup and about SeaWorld's animal rescue program. Meanwhile, Kevin uses the cellular phone to let fellow animal care experts at SeaWorld know what kind of first aid the animal will need upon arrival.

At the park, animal care experts assign the pup number 0019. They weigh it and identify it as a female. They estimate it to be one of this year's pups, probably only a few months old.

The first order of treatment is tube-feeding an electrolyte solution—the animal equivalent of Gatorade®. The solution has already been prepared. While Kevin kneels over the 33-kg (73-lb.) pup to steady it, Jody gently pushes a long clear tube through the pup's mouth and down into its stomach. She inserts a large syringe to the exposed end of the tube and squirts electrolyte solution directly into the pup's stomach.

"We'll give it 700 milliliters of electrolyte solution twice more today," says Jody. "Restoring fluids is the most important thing right now. Then we'll assess where to go next."

Eight weeks later...

Rest, fluids, and a steady diet of fish have given elephant seal pup 0019 a second chance. She is now eating on her own—about 7 kg (15 lb.) of fish each day. Healthy and active, she's gained more than 22 kg (49 lb.), and she's ready for release.

"Look at her eyes," says Kevin. They are bright and wet. Her ribs no longer show; they're covered with a thick layer of blubber. Kevin attaches a bright orange tag to a hind flipper, guides her into a transport unit, and carefully records her weight. Then Jody attaches the transport unit to a crane and lowers her into the waiting release boat, captained by SeaWorld Assistant Curator Keith Yip. The team goes through the same routine with another rehabilitated seal.

With the seals safely aboard, Keith heads for open ocean. Ten miles out, he opens the transport unit. Without fanfare, the seals slip quietly into the sea and disappear.

The SeaWorld animal rescue team gently places an Atlantic bottlenose dolphin *(Tursiops truncatus)* in a specially designed stretcher for transport to SeaWorld Orlando for treatment.

First aid for stranded animals

SeaWorld animal care specialists respond to calls reporting possible strandings. At the scene, SeaWorld rescuers examine a stranded animal for external injuries. They check and monitor the animal's vital signs including body temperature, heart rate, and respiratory rate. Depending on the species and the condition of the animal, they may apply water, ice, ointments, and wet sheets and towels to protect the animal from wind and sun and to prevent it from overheating. They may assist an animal in keeping its blowhole or nostrils and eyes free of water and sand.

Transporting stranded animals requires expertise. Handling large, wild animals, even if they are debilitated, can be hazardous, and SeaWorld and Busch Gardens animal care specialists are trained to know how to approach and recover stranded animals. Knowing that any interaction with humans can be stressful for a wild animal, they take special care to prevent animals from injuring themselves further. Seals and sea lions are transported in cages designed to restrict movement. Whales, dolphins, and manatees are lifted with strong nylon slings or specially-designed stretchers and transported on thick layers of foam rubber.

Some stranded animals are brought to SeaWorld or Busch Gardens by agencies such as state Fish and Game departments, the U.S. Fish and Wildlife Service (USFWS), or marine mammal stranding network volunteers. Private citizens who find ill or injured birds often bring them to SeaWorld.

SeaWorld animal rescue specialists are trained to safely approach and recover stranded animals such as this elephant seal pup.

Medical attention

Upon arrival at SeaWorld, a rescued animal is examined by veterinarians and animal care specialists. Medical technologists may analyze blood, stool, and urine samples to help pinpoint specific trouble areas.

Veterinarians can take x-rays, administer antibiotics, and perform surgery such as suturing wounds and repairing fractures. If an animal is injured, the staff may also analyze bacterial cultures taken from wounds.

SeaWorld and Busch Gardens parks have facilities equipped to rehabilitate stranded animals. Facilities include a laboratory, surgical suite, food preparation room, and recovery areas.

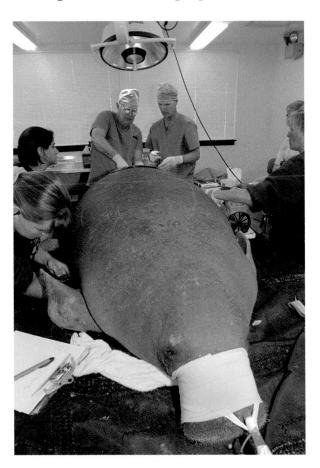

Surgical suite.

The surgical suite may include an x-ray machine, anesthesia equipment with a ventilator, and a surgery table. Veterinarians sometimes also use specialized diagnostic tools such as ultrasound machines and endoscopy equipment (scopes for seeing inside an animal's body).

At SeaWorld Orlando, a large manatee undergoes surgery under anesthesia to repair deep propeller wounds.

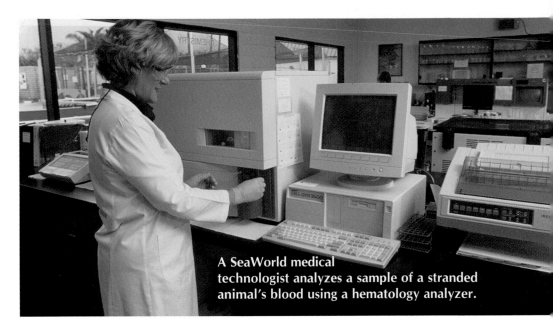

A SeaWorld medical technologist analyzes a sample of a stranded animal's blood using a hematology analyzer.

Laboratory.

SeaWorld laboratories are equipped with the latest automated instruments to perform laboratory tests on rescued animals. An automated hematology (blood) analyzer counts red blood cells, white blood cells, and platelets. A laser beam counts and differentiates white blood cells. Laboratory technologists can detect and observe blood cells, bacteria, and parasites under microscopes that magnify objects up to 1,000 times their actual size.

To ensure that animal environments are healthy and clean, laboratory technologists test water from each animal pool every day.

A pharmacy holds antibiotics, intravenous fluids, and other medications as well as vitamins formulated for marine mammals, fishes, and birds.

A SeaWorld medical technologist dispenses vitamins and medications.

SeaWorld animal care specialists tube-feed a rescued, orphaned pygmy sperm whale *(Kogia breviceps).*

Food preparation room.

The food preparation room is outfitted with a freezer, thawing sinks, grinders, blenders, stomach tubes, and nursing bottles to accommodate animals requiring special diets, bottle feeding, or tube feeding.

Recovery areas.

After treatment, rescued animals recover in appropriate holding pools and enclosures suited to their specific needs.

Nourishment and hydration

Most stranded animals are severely dehydrated and grossly undernourished—often 30% to 40% below their normal weight. After a physical examination and blood analysis, the next step in treating stranded animals is to overcome dehydration and restore normal body weight. Some animals will eat on their own; others must be tube-fed essential nutrients in liquid form.

To feed animals that refuse to eat, animal care specialists use a funnel (for large animals) or a syringe (for small animals) attached to plastic tubing. The tubing is gently inserted through the animal's mouth to its stomach, then formula is poured into the funnel or injected into the tube via the syringe.

Treating young animals

Orphaned pups or calves that are still nursing are fed formula. SeaWorld uses an artificial milk replacer as the base for marine mammal formula that is generally about 13% fat and 7% protein. To meet the nutritional needs of individual animals, animal care staff may add balanced electrolyte solutions, dextrose, salmon oil, heavy whipping cream, fish, or other supplemental ingredients.

An animal care specialist bottlefeeds two hand-raised, orphaned manatees.

Baby Formula for a Whale

One of SeaWorld's best-known stranded animals was J.J., a newborn gray whale that washed ashore on a Southern California beach and was brought to SeaWorld San Diego January 11, 1997. SeaWorld veterinarians developed a formula for J.J., consisting of the following components (amounts listed are per 1 liter of formula):

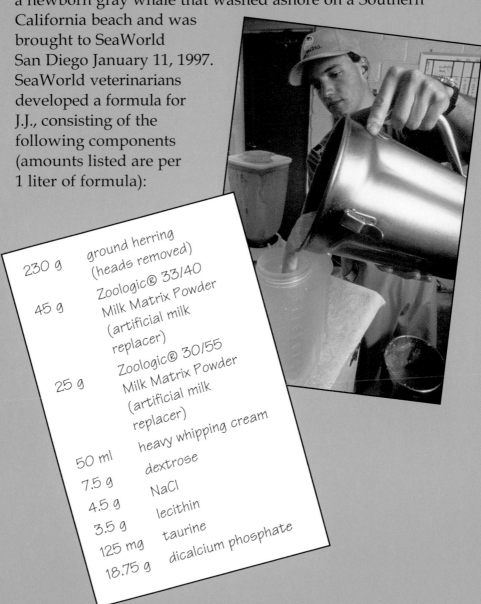

230 g	ground herring (heads removed)
45 g	Zoologic® 33/40 Milk Matrix Powder (artificial milk replacer)
25 g	Zoologic® 30/55 Milk Matrix Powder (artificial milk replacer)
50 ml	heavy whipping cream
7.5 g	dextrose
4.5 g	NaCl
3.5 g	lecithin
125 mg	taurine
18.75 g	dicalcium phosphate

In the beginning, J.J. was fed every three hours, around the clock. While one group of animal care specialists created the formula, another group donned wet suits and climbed into the

pool with the whale. Coordinating their efforts, animal care specialists surrounded the calf and gently supported her. They placed a feeding tube through her mouth and into her stomach. With a large funnel in place at the end of the tube, the formula (warmed to body temperature) was slowly poured down the tube into the whale's stomach.

J.J. quickly learned to swim directly to an animal care specialist for food and even to accept a nursing device devised by SeaWorld animal care specialists. Just eight days after her rescue, J.J. could nurse on her own with the help of just one person. Animal care specialists transitioned from feeding her in the water to feeding her at the edge of the pool, and J.J. soon responded to a "feeding call"—a tap on the surface of the water—and took the feeding tube on her own. At first, J.J. consumed 7.6 liters (2 gal.) of formula, seven times per day. Over time, her food intake increased. For the last few months before she was weaned, J.J.'s daily food intake consisted of six 20-liter (5.3-gal.) feedings per day.

(Zoologic® is a product of Pet-Ag, Inc., 201 Keyes Ave., Hampshire, IL, 60140)

Rehabilitation experts

SeaWorld and Busch Gardens veterinarians diagnose and treat marine mammals, birds, and turtles. Park medical technologists, animal care specialists, aviculturists, and aquarists play key roles in restoring health to stranded animals.

Animal Care departments transport, maintain, and manage resident and rescued marine mammals. Positions include animal care specialists, veterinarians, and medical technologists.

Aquarium departments care for SeaWorld's collection of sharks and other fishes, invertebrates, and turtles. Aquarists are responsible for the rehabilitation of sea turtles.

Aviculture departments care for SeaWorld's and Busch Gardens' birds, including penguins, parrots, flamingos, and the waterfowl collection. Aviculturists are also responsible for rehabilitation of rescued birds.

A SeaWorld aquarist weighs a loggerhead sea turtle (*Caretta caretta*) hatchling.

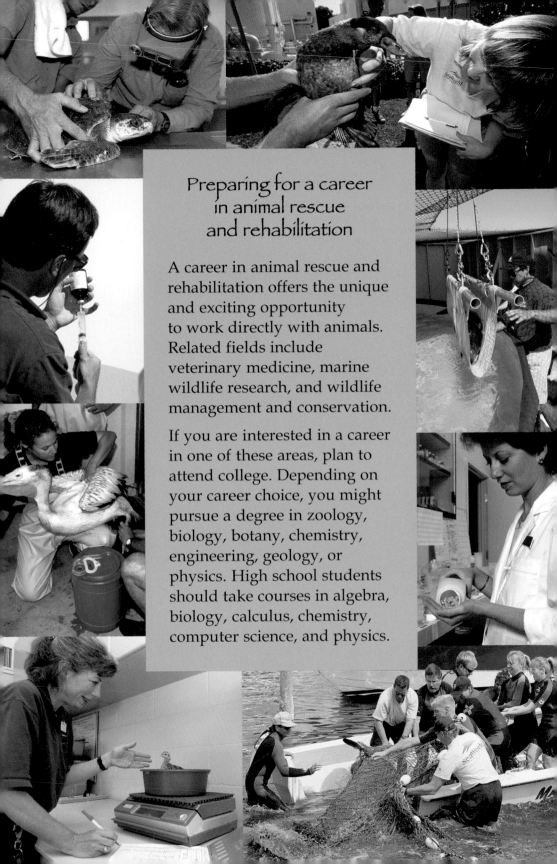

Preparing for a career in animal rescue and rehabilitation

A career in animal rescue and rehabilitation offers the unique and exciting opportunity to work directly with animals. Related fields include veterinary medicine, marine wildlife research, and wildlife management and conservation.

If you are interested in a career in one of these areas, plan to attend college. Depending on your career choice, you might pursue a degree in zoology, biology, botany, chemistry, engineering, geology, or physics. High school students should take courses in algebra, biology, calculus, chemistry, computer science, and physics.

Profile: Animal Care Specialist Jody Westberg

What made you choose this line of work?

I visited SeaWorld as a kid, and as soon as I saw the dolphins I knew that one day I wanted a job taking care of them.

What do you like best about your job?

I love the animals. They make the hard work worthwhile. I also like educating park visitors; conservation is very important to me.

What's your most memorable experience rehabilitating an animal?

A group of kids used to come visit J.J. every week or so while she was here. One day shortly before J.J. was released, I was scuba diving in her pool, cleaning up uneaten food. On this particular day I noticed these kids taping cards to the glass along the pool where J.J. (and I) could see them. I swam close enough to read the cards, and they were all farewell cards for J.J., saying goodbye and good luck. That was very touching.

How physically demanding is your job?

My job is a lot of fun, but it's also a lot of hard work. Every day we distribute about 5,000 pounds of fish to the animals throughout the park. That means I have to be able to carry 30-pound buckets of fish and ice. When I'm done, it's time to break out more food and start thawing it for the next day. We also do a lot of cleaning up after the animals. And some rescued animals may require 24-hour watch, so we do spend some long days and nights outside—in all kinds of weather.

What's the hardest part of your job?

The animals can't tell us what they need, so we have to figure out what treatment is best for each individual. Of course, the veterinarians always have the final say.

Is it hard to say goodbye to an animal that you've cared for?

Sure it is, but you always know that release is the goal. And when you've seen a truly sick animal come in, and you've cared for it and nursed it back to health, it's a great feeling to return it to its home in the sea.

What advice do you have for someone who would like to work with marine mammals as a career?

Get as much animal experience as you can, whether it's with marine animals or other animals. Even if you live in a land-locked area you can get experience caring for pets, volunteering at animal shelters, and through local 4-H clubs. I grew up on a ranch in South Dakota, so I had lots of experience working with large animals, and that really helped prepare me for my job here. In school, study biology and psychology, and if your desire is to work in an adventure park like SeaWorld, get some experience in public speaking and drama, too, so you'll be comfortable talking to groups of children and to park guests.

Jody bottlefeeds an orphaned harbor seal pup.

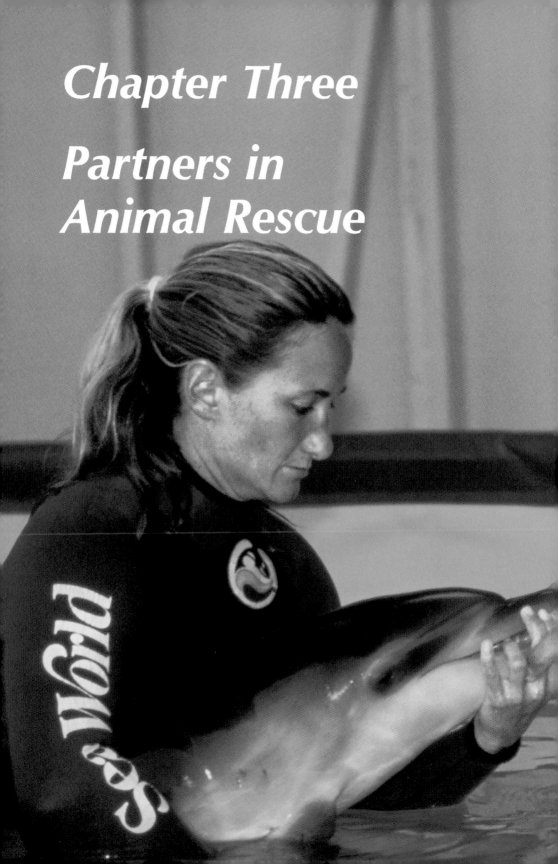

Chapter Three

Partners in
Animal Rescue

"The greatness of a nation and its moral progress can be judged by the way its animals are treated."

Mohandas Gandhi

Two rehabilitated manatees are released. Both were orphans hand-raised by SeaWorld Orlando animal care specialists for several years.

Working together to help wildlife

SeaWorld and Busch Gardens parks work hand-in-hand with federal, state, and local agencies to retrieve stranded animals and also to release rehabilitated animals. The National Marine Fisheries Service (NMFS), USFWS, the Coast Guard, state fish and game departments, wildlife conservation groups, municipal authorities, and local police and lifeguards often play critical roles in animal rescue and release.

The SeaWorld and Busch Gardens animal rescue teams follow strict regulations regarding wildlife rescue and rehabilitation. All activities concerning wild animals in the United States are governed federally by the USFWS under the U.S. Department of the Interior and NMFS under the U.S. Department of Commerce.

Some marine animals—including California sea otters, Florida manatees, some seabirds, many whale species, and all species of sea turtles—are protected by the Endangered Species Act of 1973. This Act prohibits taking, importing, or exporting any species designated as endangered by the Secretary of the Interior.

All marine mammals in U.S. waters, including stranded animals, are protected by the Marine Mammal Protection Act (MMPA) of 1972. This Act—with certain limited exemptions including public display and research—prohibits the taking and importing of marine mammals and marine mammal parts and products. The MMPA is jointly administered by the USFWS and the NMFS.

USFWS is responsible for activities concerning wild birds and non-marine mammals as well as walruses, sea otters, polar bears, dugongs, and manatees. All native birds in the U.S. are protected by the Migratory Bird Act. The USFWS issues SeaWorld and Busch Gardens parks "Special Purpose" permits for rescuing and rehabilitating wild birds.

NMFS regulates activities concerning whales, dolphins, porpoises, seals, and sea lions. NMFS has issued letters of authorization to the SeaWorld parks in California, Florida, and Texas that allow them to rescue and rehabilitate these stranded marine mammals.

In addition to the federal regulations governing stranded animals, some state governments require permits for rescuing and rehabilitating certain animals. All SeaWorld and Busch Gardens parks that rescue such animals hold the necessary permits to do so.

National Marine Mammal Health and Stranding Response Program

NMFS coordinates the National Marine Mammal Health and Stranding Response Program, which includes four components: the National Marine Mammal Tissue Bank, the Marine Mammal Stranding Network, a monitoring component, and a quality assurance program.

Marine Mammal Tissue Bank.

Scientists use standardized procedures to prepare and store tissue specimens—usually of the blubber and liver—of certain species of stranded marine mammals that die. Such specimens are held in deep-freeze at the National Marine Mammal Tissue Bank at the National Institute of Standards and Technology. These tissue samples can be used to evaluate the condition of the animal at the time of death, helping to document long-term trends in environmental quality, and may provide valuable material for future studies.

Stranding Network.

Marine mammal stranding networks within each NMFS region each have a stranding coordinator and one or more stranding operations centers. Regional Stranding

SeaWorld animal care specialists tube-feed a rescued common dolphin calf.

SeaWorld animal care specialists measure a rescued common dolphin upon its arrival at SeaWorld.

Networks are composed of volunteers who hold Letters of Authorization issued by NMFS. They include scientists, wildlife rehabilitation centers, veterinarians, wildlife management specialists, aquariums, and marinelife parks. Network members are required to collect basic biological data on each individual they rescue. SeaWorld parks are part of regional Marine Mammal Stranding Networks.

Monitoring.

The Monitoring component of the MMHSRP is charged with documenting the baseline concentrations of chemical contaminants, biochemical components, and biotoxins in stranded marine mammals.

Quality assurance.

The goal of the MMHSRP's Quality Assurance component is to develop methods to ensure the accuracy and precision of chemical analyses and tissue samples.

The Oiled Wildlife Care Center at SeaWorld San Diego is one of five regional oiled wildlife rescue and rehabilitation centers developed by the California Oiled Wildlife Care Network.

Oiled Wildlife Care at SeaWorld San Diego

In 1999, the California Department of Fish and Game and the University of California, Davis joined SeaWorld San Diego in breaking ground for a new Oiled Wildlife Care Center. The 242-square-meter (2,600-ft.^{2}) facility is designed to care for up to 200 oiled seabirds in the event of an oil spill along the Southern California coast. It is one of five regional oiled wildlife rescue and rehabilitation facilities developed by the Oiled Wildlife Care Network and one of 21 participating organizations statewide.

SeaWorld's Oiled Wildlife Care Center is an example of private and public partnership for environmental stewardship. It is a joint effort of the California Department of Fish and Game's Office of Oil Spill Prevention and Response, the University of California Davis School of Veterinary Medicine's Wildlife Health Center (which administers the Oiled Wildlife Care Network), the major oil companies doing business in California, and SeaWorld San Diego. The facility is a testament to lessons learned from past oil spills and improvements in oiled wildlife rescue, care, and rehabilitation.

When not being used for oil spill response, the center is home to SeaWorld's ongoing animal rehabilitation programs, primarily for seabirds such as pelicans, cormorants, and shorebirds.

When the Oiled Wildlife Care Center isn't being used for oil spill response it is available for other animals undergoing rehabilitation. Here a SeaWorld aviculturist administers fluids to an ill pelican.

Florida Fish and Wildlife Conservation Commission and SeaWorld Orlando

The Florida Fish and Wildlife Conservation Commission's Marine Turtle Program rescues stranded sea turtles, and state officials often call on SeaWorld Orlando for help. Rescued turtles are transported to SeaWorld Orlando for rehabilitation and released when they are healthy.

Just before release, this rehabilitated manatee is fitted with a satellite tag. The tag sends a signal to a satellite, which records information that allows scientists to track the manatee.

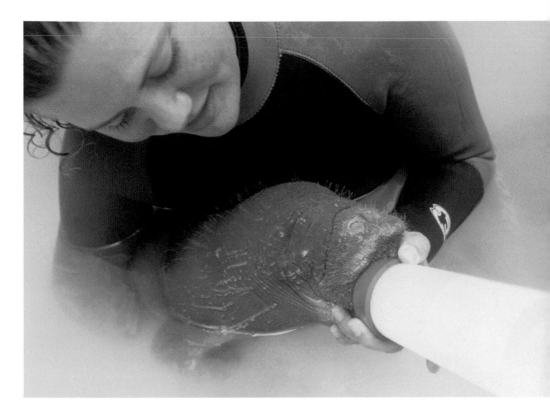

The manatee care team works around the clock for several months during the hand-rearing process. Just to teach an orphaned manatee calf to drink from a bottle takes days and sometimes weeks. Here a SeaWorld animal care specialist bottlefeeds an orphaned manatee.

The Florida Manatee Sanctuary Act of 1978 protects the endangered Florida manatee from harm and harassment. In cooperation with the USFWS, the Act sets up refuges, establishes boat speed zones, and oversees other areas of human/manatee interaction. The state of Florida distributes some funding for the rescue and rehabilitation of stranded manatees.

SeaWorld Orlando is one of only three centers authorized by the USFWS to rescue and rehabilitate ill, injured, and orphaned manatees. A small portion of state funding goes to the Orlando park to help offset the substantial cost of manatee rescue and rehabilitation. SeaWorld Orlando has provided critical life-saving intervention for hundreds of manatees.

Guests at SeaWorld San Diego interact with Shamu® and friends. At SeaWorld and Busch Gardens parks, guests are entertained and educated, and they also help fund marine mammal conservation and rescue programs.

SeaWorld and Busch Gardens guests: partners in conservation

Rescuing and rehabilitating animals is an expensive endeavor. While SeaWorld Orlando receives some funding from the State of Florida for manatee rescue and rehabilitation (see page 49), these funds don't come close to paying the full bill. Expenses of the SeaWorld/Busch Gardens Animal Rescue and Rehabilitation Program, including staff, transportation, and facilities, add up to well over $1 million per year.

The SeaWorld/Busch Gardens Animal Rescue and Rehabilitation Program, along with countless other environmental conservation and wildlife protection projects that SeaWorld and Busch Gardens support, is possible only because of the people who visit the parks. Just by walking through the parks' front gates, guests essentially "fund" the parks' global conservation efforts.

A young guest at SeaWorld San Diego comes face to face with a polar bear (Ursus maritimus).

Chapter Four

Rescued Animals

*"One touch of
nature makes the
whole world kin."*

William Shakespeare,
Troilus and Cressida

After being hit by a car and losing a wing, Emma, a screech owl *(Otus asio)* arrived at Busch Gardens Tampa Bay in 1996 for rehabilitation. Today Emma helps educate people about owl conservation.

So many animals...

Since the inception of the Animal Rescue and Rehabilitation program in 1965, more than 12,000 stranded animals have been rescued by or brought to SeaWorld and Busch Gardens parks for treatment and rehabilitation.

Weather conditions, food availability, animal population levels, breeding success, and other factors influence the number of animals that strand in a given year. Each year for the past ten years, SeaWorld and Busch Gardens rescued between 304 and 872 birds, between five and 23 cetaceans (whales and dolphins), between 11 and 30 manatees, between 59 and 449 pinnipeds (seals, sea lions, and walruses), between 16 and 109 turtles, and as many as ten sea otters. So far 1998 has been the busiest year for the program; park animal rescue and rehabilitation specialists treated 1,310 animals.

Hawks and herons. Owls and ospreys. Cormorants and cranes. Geese and grebes. Ill, injured, or blown off course, hundreds of birds are rescued and rehabilitated at SeaWorld and Busch Gardens each year. Ducks, egrets, terns, and storks also are among the birds that wind up at SeaWorld or Busch Gardens parks in need of help.

At SeaWorld San Diego, aviculturists have rehabilitated hundreds of California brown pelicans, an endangered species that at one time faced extinction. Each year 50 or more of the birds are rehabilitated at the San Diego park. In 1992 an El Niño condition and associated storms made foraging difficult for juvenile birds that had just fledged, and SeaWorld San Diego rescued 240 brown pelicans, of which 104 were successfully rehabilitated and released.

Since 1996 SeaWorld San Diego has partnered with USFWS to assist with the medical care and rehabilitation of brown and white pelicans (*P. erythrorhynchos*) suffering from suspected botulism poisoning. Care and treatment consists of

When the USFWS in Alaska confiscated more than 100 eider eggs from poachers, they flew the eggs to SeaWorld Cleveland. There aviculturists hand-raised the eider chicks.

SeaWorld bird experts teamed with the USFWS to rehabilitate white pelicans suffering from suspected botulism poisoning. Here a rehabilitated white pelican is released in San Diego County.

administering fluids, nutrients, and medication and giving supportive care until the toxin is flushed from the birds' systems. Rehabilitation takes weeks to months, after which time the birds are released into suitable habitat in the Tijuana Estuary.

In 1993 USFWS approached SeaWorld Cleveland with more than 100 eider eggs that had been confiscated from poachers by USFWS Alaska. Eiders live in difficult-to-access arctic regions, and little was known about their populations, which many experts believe are decreasing. The eggs were in

various stages of hatching when the portable incubators were unloaded off the plane in Cleveland. SeaWorld Cleveland hatched and hand-reared the threatened spectacled eiders *(Somateria fischeri)*, king eiders *(S. spectabilis)*, and Pacific eiders *(S. mollissima)*.

In addition to the seabirds, waterfowl, and other birds rehabilitated at SeaWorld and Busch Gardens parks, as many as 1,000 small birds are rescued by or brought to the parks for triage before being placed with local qualified wildlife rehabilitation organizations.

An Osprey Named Zap

For years, Norma and Ed Roberts had enjoyed watching a pair of ospreys (*Pandion haliaetus*) that nested in a tree just behind their house in Palm Coast, Florida. Ospreys mate for life and return to the same nesting site year after year.

In 1990, the female osprey laid three eggs; five weeks later, the chicks emerged. The Roberts watched the attentive osprey parents bring bits of fish to feed their chicks.

But on June 5, during a fierce storm, a bolt of lightning struck the tree where the osprey family lived, and the tree crashed to the ground. The Roberts searched the nest to find that, amazingly, one chick was alive. The Roberts rescued the baby bird and turned it over to the USFWS.

The survivor—a female chick christened "Zap"—was hand-reared in the

photo by Norma Roberts

Busch Gardens Tampa Bay animal nursery. Ospreys don't usually fare well in captivity, but Zap thrived. Animal care specialists glove-trained the young bird and spent countless hours teaching her how to feed herself.

Today Zap is a mature osprey weighing about 1.4 kg (3 lb.). She is 51 cm (20 in.) tall and has a 1.5-m (5-ft.) wingspan. Zap participates in educational programs at Busch Gardens and has traveled throughout the U.S. and Canada making media appearances to educate the public about ospreys.

M ost of the marine mammals (approximately 85%) rescued by SeaWorld parks are seals and sea lions. SeaWorld San Diego has rescued and rehabilitated hundreds of California sea lions, northern elephant seal pups, and harbor seals *(Phoca vitulina)*. Less frequently, the San Diego park has treated Guadalupe fur seals, northern fur seals *(Callorhinus ursinus)*, ringed seals *(Phoca hispida),* and orphaned Pacific walrus *(Odobenus rosmarus divergens)* calves.

Despite its inland location, SeaWorld Cleveland played an important role in the rehabilitation of a young male hooded

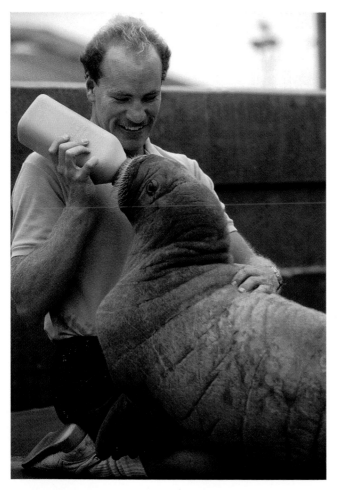

seal *(Cystophora cristata)* that stranded off the northern New England coast and was rescued by the New England Aquarium. In a cooperative effort

A SeaWorld animal care specialist bottlefeeds an orphaned walrus calf.

SeaWorld San Diego has rescued hundreds of California sea lions from San Diego beaches. First-year pups account for most stranded animals.

between institutions, the seal was moved to SeaWorld Cleveland for long-term rehabilitation. Once recovered, the seal was transported back to New England and released.

First-year pups account for most seal and sea lion strandings: about 80% of rescued seals and sea lions are less than a year old. When a seal or sea lion mother weans her pup, she leaves the pup to fend for itself. Pups unsuccessful at foraging on their own cannot survive this weaning process, and mortality for wild seal and sea lion pups may be as high as 20% to 50% in their first year.

The increased storm activity and reduced prey associated with an El Niño make foraging even harder for seals and sea lions, and more of these animals strand in an El Niño year. SeaWorld San Diego rescued 449 seals and sea lions in 1998 and 472 seals and sea lions in 1983—both years marked by severe El Niño conditions.

Turtles

On a cold December day in 1989, marine patrol officers found nearly a hundred green sea turtles *(Chelonia mydas)* floating in a semi-dormant state at the surface in Florida's Indian River Lagoon. Low water temperature had slowed the sea turtles' metabolism, making them sluggish and unable to feed. The hypothermic turtles were rescued and housed in recovery pools at SeaWorld Orlando for about 10 weeks. When the water in Indian River Lagoon warmed up, the healthy turtles were released back into the same area.

Each year SeaWorld parks treat dozens of green, loggerhead, hawksbill *(Eretmochelys imbricata)*, Kemp's ridley *(Lepidochelys kempi)*, and leatherback *(Dermochelys coriacea)* sea turtles—all endangered or threatened species. Some turtles are rescued with injuries resulting from entanglement, watercraft collisions,

Dozens of endangered green sea turtles are rehabilitated at SeaWorld.

ocean dredging, or ingestion of non-food items. Injured and ill turtles may require round-the-clock care and months of treatment and rehabilitation.

Some green sea turtles strand when abnormal, lobed, tumorous growths called fibropapillomas threaten their survival. These growths appear between the scales and scutes, on the eyes and eyelids, in the mouth, on abdominal organs, on the back of the neck, and where the flippers meet the trunk. Fibropapillomas ultimately can be life threatening to free-ranging sea turtles by obscuring their vision and affecting their ability to feed, by becoming large enough to impair normal swimming, by interfering with respiration, or by predisposing them to secondary infections.

In addition to caring for stranded sea turtles, aquarists at SeaWorld Orlando have rescued and rehabilitated ill or injured Florida gopher tortoises (Gopherus polyphemus). Sometimes the tortoises have fractured shells that require medical treatment.

SeaWorld aquarists release a rehabilitated loggerhead sea turtle into the ocean off San Diego. The attached satellite transmitter will allow scientists at Hubbs-SeaWorld Research Institute to track the turtle's movements at sea.

Wrong-Way Corrigan

Green sea turtles typically are found along the west coast of North and South America from California to Ecuador. So when two hunters found a green sea turtle thousands of kilometers off course near Montague Island, Alaska in October 1996, they knew the animal was in danger. They rescued the malnourished turtle and took it to authorities in Cordova, Alaska.

NMFS shipped the sea turtle to researcher and conservationist Dr. Scott Eckert of the Hubbs-SeaWorld Research Institute in San Diego. (A baggage manager at the San Diego airport dubbed the turtle, "Wrong-Way Corrigan" after a pilot who flew from New York to Ireland in 1938.) Dr. Eckert turned the sea turtle over to SeaWorld San Diego veterinarians and aquarists for rehabilitation.

Upon its arrival, SeaWorld veterinarians examined the turtle's blood and administered fluids. For the next nine months, SeaWorld aquarists monitored the sea turtle and fed it fish, squid, shrimp, vitamins, and minerals. In nine months of rehabilitation at SeaWorld San Diego, Wrong-Way Corrigan gained about 18 kg (40 lb.).

"The turtle had regained its health by March, yet the ocean temperature wasn't warm enough for it to be released," said Dr. Eckert.

When ocean waters warmed up in July, Wrong-Way Corrigan was released off San Diego. Before the release, Dr. Eckert attached satellite transmitters to track the turtle's movements. Location data was picked up by satellites and sent to Dr. Eckert by email.

Unexpectedly, Wrong-Way Corrigan traveled north — the "wrong" way. "Corrigan taught us that it may be far more common than we previously thought for green sea turtles to travel north — even to Alaska," said Dr. Eckert. The wayward turtle was last tracked in late 1997... still heading north.

Cetaceans: whales and dolphins

Possibly the world's best-loved stranded animal was J.J. the gray whale. A little more than 14 months after the orphaned whale was rescued on a Southern California beach, news crews from around the world heralded SeaWorld's remarkable success at rehabilitating, raising, and releasing the baleen whale calf.

And J.J. was not SeaWorld's first successfully rehabilitated baleen whale. In late November 1989, SeaWorld Orlando animal care specialists rescued a 2,270-kg (5,000-lb.) Bryde's whale *(Balaenoptera edeni)* stranded on a beach near Clearwater, Florida. After six weeks of treatment and round-the-clock care, the huge baleen whale was successfully released back into the Atlantic Ocean.

According to NMFS, bottlenose dolphins, pygmy sperm whales, and common dolphins are among the most common stranded cetaceans in the United States. SeaWorld parks have rescued these species as well as Risso's dolphins *(Grampus griseus)*, Pacific white-sided dolphins *(Lagenorhynchus obliquidens),*

A SeaWorld animal care specialist helps support a rescued pygmy sperm whale. The young female whale stranded in San Diego in 1999.

An animal care specialist supports and guides a rescued Bryde's whale at SeaWorld Orlando.

spinner and spotted dolphins *(Stenella* spp.), a northern right whale dolphin *(Lissodelphis borealis)*, killer whales *(Orcinus orca)*, false killer whales *(Pseudorca crassidens)*, pygmy killer whales *(Feresa attenuata)*, pilot whales, sperm whales *(Physeter macrocephalus)*, and dwarf sperm whales *(Kogia simus)*.

SeaWorld Orlando has participated in rescue efforts for mass-stranded pilot whales and false killer whales. Sadly, none of the mass-stranded whales survived; however, animal care experts were able to collect valuable data that may help scientists to better understand why whales strand.

This rescued manatee suffered from broken ribs and a punctured lung, which made regulating buoyancy difficult. Here animal care specialists attach a specially designed and constructed flotation device that will make swimming and floating easier while the animal recovers.

Manatees

Slow-swimming, gentle plant-eaters, manatees live in the warm, shallow waters of Florida's rivers, bays, canals, estuaries, and coastal areas rich in seagrass and other vegetation. Alarmingly, studies suggest that the Florida manatee population continues to decline. Mortality counts suggest that as much as 11% of the manatee population in Florida may have died every year since 1984.

From 1990 through 1999, 30% of manatee deaths in Florida were caused by human-related factors. Collisions with boats and barges is the largest human-related cause of death,

Dead men tell no tales. Dead manatees yield data.

From 1974 to 1986, SeaWorld Orlando participated in a manatee carcass salvage program in which SeaWorld staff retrieved and examined dead manatees. The staff recorded such information as morphological characteristics, reproductive status, and cause of death. This information is archived by the State of Florida and SeaWorld Orlando for future manatee studies.

accounting for 23% of all manatees that died in Florida waters (1990–1999). Entrapment in flood control gates and navigation locks is the second leading human-related cause of death.

Scientists and volunteers are battling to save manatees from extinction. In 1977 SeaWorld Orlando rescued and rehabilitated its first injured manatee. SeaWorld Orlando has rescued more than 250 manatees in distress, and has released more than 100 rehabilitated manatees. Many of the stranded manatees are orphaned or ill animals, while others have injuries from crab trap lines, shrimp nets, fishing lines, flood gates, or watercraft.

In 1998 SeaWorld San Diego opened its *Manatee Rescue* habitat, providing additional long-term rehabilitation and housing for animals that are unsuitable for release. Moving manatees to San Diego freed space at SeaWorld Orlando for manatees in need of acute medical care.

Human intervention is critical for manatee conservation. "People created the problem," said Daniel K. Odell, Ph.D., SeaWorld/Busch Gardens research biologist and co-author of the book, *Manatees and Dugongs.* "People have to take the necessary steps to protect them. It's up to us to work together to get the manatee off the Endangered Species List." Integral to manatee conservation since 1974, Odell received a Presidential Point of Light Award from former U.S. president George Bush in 1990 for his work with stranded animals.

SeaWorld Orlando and SeaWorld Cleveland sometimes rescue orphaned North American river otter *(Lutra canadensis)* pups. Otter pups are bottlefed before being weaned to a diet of fish, then eventually released.

California sea otters *(Enhydra lutris nereis)* sometimes strand along the coast of central California. When nearby rehabilitation centers need help, they occasionally send rescued sea otters to SeaWorld San Diego for special care and rehabilitation.

SeaWorld San Diego also participated in the rehabilitation of Alaska sea otters *(E. l. lutris)* that were soiled by highly toxic

crude oil as a result of the 1989 *Exxon Valdez* oil spill. Scientists from the Hubbs-SeaWorld Research Institute,

A SeaWorld animal care specialist hand-feeds an Alaska sea otter that was rescued following the 1989 *Exxon Valdez* oil spill in Alaska.

When rehabilitation centers in central California need help raising orphaned sea otters, they occasionally send rescued otter pups to SeaWorld San Diego.

in cooperation with other facilities and volunteers, coordinated efforts to rescue and treat the oiled sea otters.

Crude oil destroyed the water repellency and insulative qualities of the otters' fur. Scientists removed the crude oil with dishwashing detergent. As a result of crude oil ingestion, many otters experienced anemia, shock, seizures, and hypoglycemia (low blood sugar), as well as damage to several internal organs. The toxic hydrocarbons in the crude oil were particularly damaging to the liver. Scientists administered a treatment of activated charcoal, given orally, to bind to the hydrocarbons in the intestine and allow them to pass.

The affected Alaska sea otters then required a long rehabilitation period to regain the natural oils that protect their fur and the layer of air that insulates them. Of 360 otters that were rescued and treated at nearby rehabilitation facilities, 195 were successfully rehabilitated and released. At the request of USFWS, some rescued sea otters were monitored long-term in zoological parks such as SeaWorld San Diego.

Chapter Five
Back to Sea

"All the flowers of all the tomorrows are in the seeds of today."

Chinese proverb

The main objective of the SeaWorld/Busch Gardens Animal Rescue and Rehabilitation Program is to return rehabilitated animals to the wild, and thousands of healthy marine mammals, birds, and turtles have been released following rehabilitation at SeaWorld and Busch Gardens parks.

When a rehabilitated animal is healthy, strong, and able to fend for itself in the wild, it is ready for release. Marine animals are transported to sea aboard a boat, accompanied by SeaWorld animal care specialists. Either by boat or by air, the animal care specialists search for other animals of the same species. When they spot a group of animals at sea, they release the rehabilitated animal in that vicinity. Then they remain at the release site long enough to confirm that the released animal swims, breathes, and behaves in a manner typical for the species, indicating that the animal should be able to survive in the wild.

A SeaWorld animal care specialist releases rehabilitated California sea lions.

In 1994 and 1995, several common dolphins stranded on the central California coast. Six were rehabilitated at SeaWorld San Diego and released. Here animal care specialists load a rehabilitated dolphin onto a release boat.

Before a rehabilitated marine mammal can be returned to the ocean, it must meet criteria for release established by NMFS or USFWS. NMFS has established the following criteria for releasing a rehabilitated whale, dolphin, seal or sea lion:

◆ The animal is eating well.

◆ The animal exhibits good weight gain and/or is able to maintain healthy body weight.

◆ Behavioral activity is normal: the animal exhibits a variable swimming repertoire, normal feeding behavior, and normal breathing patterns.

◆ The animal exhibits stable or improving blood values that are compatible with survival in the wild.

◆ The animal has been marked for future identification.

Farewell to J.J.

J.J. the gray whale was the largest animal ever to be returned to the wild. Her release was timed to coincide with the northward migration of gray whales, which pass San Diego on their way from the lagoons of Baja California to feeding grounds in Alaska. Getting the immense mammal from SeaWorld San Diego to the ocean required a great deal of teamwork

At SeaWorld, a crane slowly lifted J.J. out of her pool and placed her carefully inside a 12-m (39-ft.), foam-lined steel transport unit aboard a flatbed truck. Escorted by San Diego Police, the truck departed for San Diego Naval Station. At the Naval Station, a calm J.J. was again lifted out of her transport unit and placed on thick foam pads on the deck of the Coast Guard vessel *Conifer*. With J.J. aboard, the ship headed for

open ocean. At every step of the journey, SeaWorld animal care specialists were on hand to keep J.J. wet and comfortable.

About 3.2 km (2 mi.) off the coast of San Diego, the *Conifer's* cargo boom lifted J.J.'s sling over the water and released the whale into the Pacific Ocean. The animal care specialists who had cared for J.J. for the past 14 months cheered as the world's best-known gray whale began her new life in the sea.

NMFS requires rehabilitated marine mammals to be tagged or marked before release. A SeaWorld animal care specialist attaches a NMFS tag to the flipper of each seal, sea lion, and sea turtle before it is released. Cryogenic markings ("freeze-brands") are another way to identify released animals. Manatees, whales, and dolphins are usually marked cryogenically before release. In addition, certain animals may be candidates for satellite or radio transmitters or for Passive Integrated Transponder (PIT) tags.

PIT tags are widely used in fisheries and wildlife research. A PIT tag is a microchip enclosed in a tiny glass capsule, which is injected into an animal. Each PIT tag is coded with data including a unique identification code. Tag codes and data are entered into a computer database when the animal is first tagged. Later, when the tag is detected, a reader device electronically records the identification code and data.

(Above) an orange NMFS tag marks this elephant seal's hind flipper.

(Right) A rehabilitated harbor seal awaits release.

Tracking Catalina Bob

Hubbs-SeaWorld Research Institute Senior Research Biologist Brent Stewart studies marine mammals and their ecosystems. He developed a research project that would allow him to track the movements of wild dolphins using a satellite transmitter. But first, the transmitter had to be attached to a wild dolphin.

That's why, when "Catalina Bob"—an adult male common dolphin who had been rehabilitated at SeaWorld San Diego—was released, he wore a transmitter package on his dorsal fin. NMFS authorized researchers to attach the transmitter package. The procedure was similar to getting an ear pierced: After applying local anesthetic, veterinarians placed two small pins through the dorsal fin, holding the transmitter in place. The package was designed to fall off within a few months and to break away in the unlikely event that Catalina Bob became entangled in debris at sea.

Catalina Bob awaits release. The satellite transmitter attached to his dorsal fin will allow researchers to track his movements in the ocean.

On August 25, 1994, Catalina Bob was released about 14 miles west of Mission Bay, San Diego. For the next month, his satellite transmitter sent signals to an orbiting satellite. The satellite relayed the signals to a computerized receiving station that pinpointed Catalina Bob's where-abouts within 1,000 m (0.6 mi.). Dr. Stewart was able to log onto the computer system to track the movements of Catalina Bob.

Following his release, Catalina Bob journeyed north. His last signal was picked up by satellite one month after his release—September 25, 1994—and located him near Point Sur, California. Such tracking studies help scientists learn about marine animals and their migratory behavior.

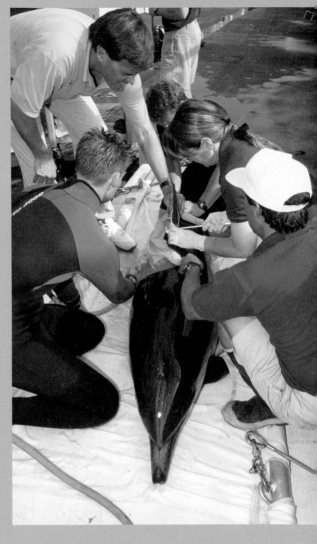

(Above) Veterinarians and animal care specialists attach a satellite transmitter to Catalina Bob.

(Left) A closer look at Catalina Bob's satellite transmitter.

Rehabilitated manatees that are not deemed releasable remain at SeaWorld for long-term care.

"Un-releasable" animals

Unfortunately, not every animal is a good candidate for release. Experts agree that a rehabilitated animal should be released only when there is a reasonable expectation that it will survive and lead a normal life. Some animals are unlikely to fare well on their own in the wild; in accordance with NMFS and USFWS regulations, such animals are not released.

Some rehabilitated animals are permanently debilitated due to injuries or as a lasting result of illness. And in some rare cases, rescued animals adapt to and become too dependent on the care of humans. Releasing such animals into a wild environment where they would face hunger, parasites, disease, and pollution would be unwise and potentially dangerous. Such animals are kept at SeaWorld or other authorized facilities, on public display or in off-exhibit habitats. They live out the remainder of their lives in a protective environment where they receive high-quality food and excellent medical care.

The eventual outcome of an animal depends upon its initial condition when rescued. Pinnipeds (seals and sea lions) have a greater recovery rate than cetaceans (whales and dolphins), in large part because cetaceans typically strand only when extremely ill or seriously injured. Juvenile animals often have a better chance of full recovery than do adults.

Releasing marine mammals that were stranded and rehabilitated is not comparable to releasing an animal that has lived in the care of humans for a long period of time. In general,

rehabilitated animals that are "releasable" have been cared for by humans for only a short time. They know how to catch food and survive in the ocean and have not grown accustomed to human care. SeaWorld animal care specialists take care to limit their interactions with rescued animals in an effort to prevent the animals from adapting to and depending on human care.

(Above) **Rehabilitated harbor seal pups are released on a San Diego beach.**

(Right) **A SeaWorld animal care specialist helps these harbor seal pups learn to catch their own live fish, limiting her interaction with them so that they don't grow accustomed to human care.**

Chapter Six
Species Conservation

"...the word of
the Lorax seems
perfectly clear.
UNLESS
someone like you
cares a whole
awful lot, nothing
is going to get
better. It's not."

Dr. Seuss,
The Lorax

"Sweet Pea" was rescued from the outflow of a sewage treatment plant in Houston, Texas and rehabilitated at SeaWorld San Antonio.

Beyond individual rescue

Rescuing individual animals can and does make a difference. Each endangered Florida manatee or California sea otter that is rescued and rehabilitated is vital to the population.

Healthy captive animal populations also can help prevent extinction through reintroduction of animals, supportive breeding, and research. To this end, the American Zoo and Aquarium Association (AZA) has developed several Species Survival Plans. The goal of a Species Survival Plan (SSP) is to preserve, in zoos and aquariums, species that are threatened or endangered in the wild. An SSP includes a species Master Plan that outlines a regional breeding strategy for the species and a Husbandry Manual that describes current techniques and potential problems in caring for the species. It is designed to be a supplement, not an alternative, to preservation in nature.

SeaWorld parks and Busch Gardens Tampa Bay are SSP Participating Institutions for the following species:

◆ addax *(Addax nasomaculatus)*

◆ Asian elephant *(Elephas maximus)*

◆ Asian small-clawed otter *(Aonyx cinerea)*

◆ Attwater's prairie chicken *(Tympanuchus cupido attwateri)*

◆ black rhinoceros *(Diceros bicornis)*

◆ chimpanzee *(Pan troglodytes)*

◆ colobus monkeys *(Colobus* spp.)

◆ great hornbill *(Buceros bicornis)*

◆ Grevy's zebra *(Equus grevyi)*

◆ Humboldt penguin *(Spheniscus humboldti)*

◆ lowland gorilla *(Gorilla gorilla gorilla)*

◆ Micronesian kingfisher *(Halcyon cinnamomina)*

◆ orangutan *(Pongo pygmaeus)*

◆ palm cockatoo *(Probosciger aterrimus)*

◆ ring-tailed lemur *(Lemur catta)*

◆ ruffed lemur *(Varecia variegata)*

◆ scimitar-horned oryx *(Oryx dammah)*

◆ thick-billed parrot *(Phynchopsitta pachyrhyncha)*

◆ wattled crane *(Bugeranus caranculatus)*

◆ white-naped crane *(Grus vipio)*

◆ white rhino *(Ceratotherium simum)*

◆ white-winged wood duck *(Cairina scutulata)*

Each SSP carefully manages the breeding of a species in order to maintain a healthy and self-sustaining captive population that is both genetically diverse and demographically stable. For native species, SSPs are often linked to USFWS Endangered Species Recovery Plans. Reintroduction projects have been successful in returning certain species to their natural places in the ecosystem.

Black Rhino SSP

An endangered species, less than 2,000 black rhinoceroses remain in their native Africa. Research and propagation at places like Busch Gardens Tampa Bay may prove to be critical for the survival of this species.

Busch Gardens Tampa Bay's Serengeti Plain is home to five black rhinos, and the park participates in the black rhino SSP program. Three rhinos are trained to voluntarily submit to routine husbandry practices, including drawing blood.

Cooperation among zoological institutions can be key to the success of an SSP. At Busch Gardens Tampa Bay, a male rhino named Jasper is the primary source for a groundbreaking baseline blood study being conducted at the San Diego Zoo. The male rhino stands willingly while rhino keepers take weekly —sometimes daily—blood samples, which are shipped via air to San Diego. Jasper's immense contribution to this research will help experts better understand diseases that affect black rhinos.

FIGs and TAGs

Busch Gardens and SeaWorld animal care specialists also participate in AZA-sponsored Fauna Interest Groups (FIGs) and Taxon Advisory Groups (TAGs).

FIGs were formed to directly involve zoos and aquariums in the preservation of native wildlife habitats and species recovery plans. FIGs help coordinate and promote the conservation activities of institutions in different geographic regions and foster cooperation with the respective foreign governments. The goals are to help establish nature reserves, generate support for existing parks, conduct vital field research, educate the public about conservation, and obtain animals for cooperative captive breeding programs.

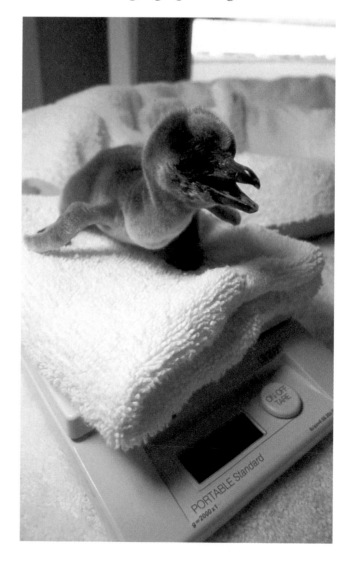

SeaWorld San Diego participates in the SSP for Humboldt penguins. Here a Humboldt penguin chick is weighed.

The American Zoo and Aquarium Association

All four SeaWorld parks and Busch Gardens Tampa Bay are accredited by the American Zoo and Aquarium Association (AZA), which represents virtually every major professionally operated zoological park, aquarium, wildlife park, and oceanarium in North America. The highest priority of the AZA is wildlife conservation.

The purpose of a TAG is to evaluate the present conditions surrounding a broad group of animals (marine mammals, for example) and then prioritize the different species in the group for possible captive programs. The high priority species are recommended for Species Survival Plans and studbooks. A TAG usually consists of a diverse group of experts, including field biologists, zoo professionals, and representatives from various conservation organizations. Busch Gardens and SeaWorld animal care specialists and veterinarians serve on TAGs for antelopes; wild cats; and a variety of bird groups including turacos, parrots, herons, egrets, flamingos, penguins, and gulls.

Busch Gardens zoo professionals participate in the TAG for parrots such as these hyacinth macaws (*Anodorhynchus hyacinthus*).

Education About Conservation

Millions of guests enjoy SeaWorld and Busch Gardens parks each year. They are entertained and educated as they encounter some of the earth's most wondrous creatures.

SeaWorld and Busch Gardens parks are committed to wildlife conservation and to education. Based on this long-term commitment, SeaWorld and Busch Gardens strive to provide an enthusiastic, imaginative, and intellectually stimulating atmosphere to help park guests and students develop a lifelong appreciation, understanding, and stewardship for our environment.

Through the SeaWorld/Busch Gardens Animal Rescue and Rehabilitation program, park experts learn a lot about animals and ecosystems. (See chapter 7, pages 92–99.) By sharing this information with students of all ages, they increase public awareness of how human actions affect animals.

Camp SeaWorld participants learn about bottlenose dolphins. More than a million students a year participate in SeaWorld and Busch Gardens education programs. Such programs include school field trips, outreach programs, day camps, and resident camps.

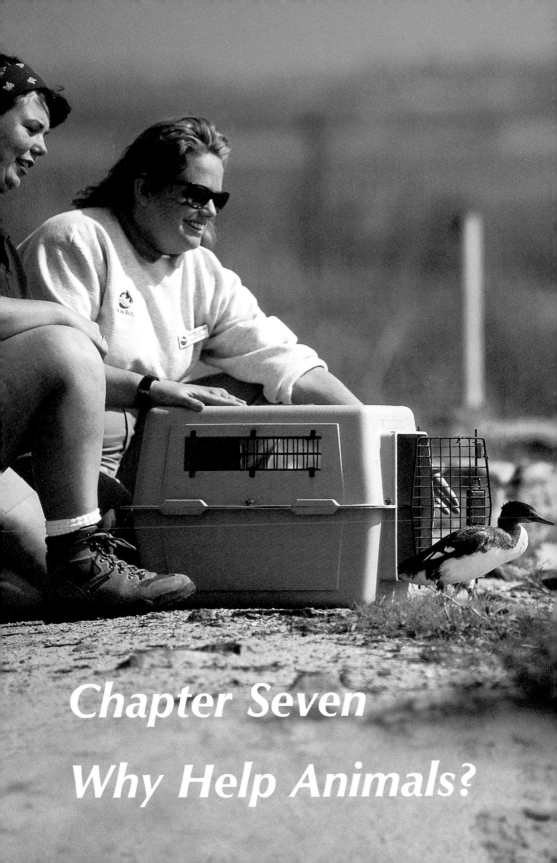

Chapter Seven

Why Help Animals?

*"We have not
inherited the
world from our
forefathers — we
have borrowed it
from our children."*

Kashmiri proverb

An animal care specialist hand-feeds a rescued northern right whale dolphin.

Helping and learning

Most people share a desire to help an animal in distress. But beyond the satisfaction of helping stranded animals, the SeaWorld/Busch Gardens Animal Rescue and Rehabilitation program offers the opportunity to learn more about wild animals.

Rescuing endangered species—such as Hawaiian monk seals *(Monachus schauinslandi)*, manatees, and sea otters—contributes directly to species conservation. And rescuing species that are plentiful—such as California sea lions and harbor seals—contributes indirectly, as scientists are able to learn more about the environment, general biology, and animal care and medicine.

Research opportunities

Studies of stranded animals provide an opportunity to gather valuable information that can't be obtained by studying wild, free-ranging individuals. This information provides insights into their species' biology and ecology.

One goal of NMFS' Marine Mammal Health and Stranding Response Program is to collect and disseminate data on the health of stranded marine mammals and health trends in wild marine mammal populations. To this end, NMFS requires stranding network members to obtain information on each stranded animal. Such information includes location of stranding and the length, condition, and sex of each stranded animal. Page 94 shows a sample stranding data sheet.

Many stranded animals do not survive, but they can provide key information that may help scientists. For example, blubber and liver samples of certain species are carefully prepared and sent to the National Marine Mammal Tissue Bank. (See page 44 for information about the Tissue Bank).

Data recovered from stranded animals helps scientists better understand features of animal biology and ecology such as—

- ◆ parasitology (the study of parasites)
- ◆ pathogens (disease-causing agents)
- ◆ physiology (how living organisms and their parts function)
- ◆ life history (how animals develop, grow, and live)
- ◆ behavior (how and why animals act the way they do)
- ◆ concentrations and possible effects of various contaminants

By observing and treating stranded animals, veterinarians and animal care specialists can study animal diseases. And animal care experts gather husbandry information and further the field of animal husbandry as they fine tune care-giving and medical procedures.

MARINE MAMMAL STRANDING REPORT

SID#_____
(NMFS USE)

FIELD NO.:_____ NMFS REGISTRATION NO.: _____

COMMON NAME: _____ GENUS: _____ SPECIES: _____

EXAMINER
Name:_____ Agency: _____ Phone: _____

Address: _____

LOCATION	TYPE OF OCCURRENCE
State: _____ County: _____	Mass Stranding: ☐ Yes ☐ No # Animals _____
City: _____	Human Interaction: ☐ Yes ☐ No ☐ ?
Locality Details: _____	Check one: ☐ 1. Boat Collision
_____	☐ 2. Shot
_____	☐ 3. Fishery Interaction
_____	☐ 4. Other _____
_____	How determined: _____
*Latitude: _____ N	Other Causes (if known): _____
*Longitude: _____ W	_____

DATE OF INITIAL OBSERVATION:	DATE OF EXAMINATION:
Yr. _____ Mo. _____ Day _____	Yr. _____ Mo. _____ Day _____
CONDITION: Check one: ☐ 1. Alive	CONDITION: Check one: ☐ 1. Alive
☐ 2. Fresh dead	☐ 2. Fresh dead
☐ 3. Moderate decomp.	☐ 3. Moderate decomp.
☐ 4. Advanced decomp.	☐ 4. Advanced decomp.
☐ 5. Mummified	☐ 5. Mummified
☐ ?. Unknown	☐ ?. Unknown

LIVE ANIMAL — Condition and Disposition:	TAGS APPLIED?: ☐ Yes ☐ No
Check one or more: ☐ 1. Released at site	TAGS PRESENT?: ☐ Yes ☐ No
☐ 2. Sick	
☐ 3. Injured	Dorsal Left Right
☐ 4. Died	
☐ 5. Euthanized	Tag No.(s): _____ _____ _____
☐ 6. Rehabilitated and released	Color (s): _____ _____ _____
☐ ?. Unknown	
	Type: _____ _____ _____
Transported to: _____	
	Placement Front/Rear Front/Rear
☐ Died ☐ Released Date: _____	

CARCASS — Disposition:	MORPHOLOGICAL DATA:
Check one: ☐ 1. Left at site	Sex — Check one: ☐ 1. Male
☐ 2. Buried	☐ 2. Female
☐ 3. Towed	☐ ?. Unknown
☐ 4. Sci. collection: (see below)	
☐ 5. Edu. collection: (see below)	Straight Length:_____ ☐ cm ☐ in ☐ est
☐ 6. Other _____	*Weight _____ ☐ kg ☐ lb ☐ est
☐ ?. Unknown	PHOTOS TAKEN? ☐ Yes ☐ No
NECROPSIED? ☐ Yes ☐ No	

REMARKS: _____

DISPOSITION OF TISSUE/SKELETAL MATERIAL: _____

NOAA Form 89-864
OMB Number: 0648-0178, expires January 31, 2000

SeaWorld animal rescue experts complete a Marine Mammal Stranding Report for each rescued animal. (This federal form is due to be revised in 2001.)

Animal care specialists at SeaWorld used what they've learned rehabilitating stranded seals to help them care for this endangered Hawaiian monk seal.

Applying what we learn

Much of the data gathered through the SeaWorld/Busch Gardens Animal Rescue and Rehabilitation Program is otherwise unavailable. It can help scientists more accurately assess population management programs in the wild and make better decisions. This information may help conserve threatened and endangered species.

In addition, the community benefits through added awareness of how human actions, both good and bad, affect animals. This awareness is the first step toward wildlife conservation and protection.

Learning From a Gray Whale

While J.J. the gray whale was undergoing rehabilitation at SeaWorld San Diego, scientists were able to add significantly to the pool of information about gray whales.

◆ Bioacoustician Dr. Ann Bowles of the Hubbs-SeaWorld Research Institute (H-SWRI) studied J.J.'s vocalizations and behavior, collecting more than 500 hours of data including "voice prints."

◆ Dr. James Sumich, a biology professor at Grossmont College in San Diego, conducted research on J.J. to determine gray whale growth, respiration, metabolic rates, and nutritional demands placed on a nursing gray whale mother. Using J.J.'s oxygen consumption rate and other data, Dr. Sumich worked on developing a mathematical formula for predicting growth rates and energy budgets in young gray whales.

◆ Dr. Sam Ridgway, Navy marine mammal veterinarian and scientist, conducted studies of J.J.'s hearing abilities.

◆ Dr. John Heyning of the Los Angeles County Museum of Natural History tested a hypothesis about how gray whales regulate body temperature by measuring the temperature of J.J.'s tongue as she was feeding (Heyning and Mead, 1997).

◆ Dr. Lev Mukhametov of Moscow, Russia and colleagues did a round-the-clock study of 24-hour rhythm in J.J. — the first such research ever conducted on a baleen whale.

If you see a stranded animal...

Do not approach a stranded animal, and do not try to return it to the water. Remember, some seals and sea lions normally haul out on land, and mothers may leave their pups for short periods of time. Stay at least 15 m (about 50 ft.) away from stranded or hauled-out animals. Wild animals—whether healthy or in need of help—can become alarmed by the presence of humans, and may bite. Also, without specific authorization through NMFS or USFWS, you are prohibited from moving marine mammals—dead or alive.

Authorized marine mammal rescue experts from SeaWorld observe a California sea lion to determine whether it is in need of help or if it is a healthy animal resting on the beach.

Here's an exception: When authorized Marine Mammal Stranding Network members are on the scene, someone may ask you for help. You may be asked to help with procedures to keep the animal comfortable or to move the animal, or to help with crowd control.

If you are first on the scene, or if the animal has not yet been reported, notify the local marine mammal rehabilitation center. Before you call, take note of some important details:

◆ Where is the animal? Be as specific as possible. If the animal is alive, time until rescue and medical attention arrive may be critical.

◆ What are the physical characteristics of the animal? Does it have any identification tags or markings? Color, size, and other characteristics will help experts determine the species and what rescue equipment and volunteers are needed.

◆ What is the condition of the animal? Is it alive or dead? In the water or on land? Are there signs of injury?

If you see a stranded marine mammal like this California sea lion, you can help by notifying the nearest marine mammal rehabilitation center, lifeguards, or animal control officers.

SeaWorld animal rescue experts rescue a sea lion pup from the beach.

If you don't know the phone number for the local marine mammal rehabilitation center, contact local lifeguards, park rangers, or animal control officers. If you are unsuccessful at reaching authorities, call the NMFS national enforcement hotline at 1-800-853-1964 and ask for the phone number of the marine mammal stranding coordinator in your area.

Glossary

anesthesia — loss of pain and other sensations, caused by certain drugs.

anesthetic — a drug that produces anesthesia.

beached animal — a dead marine animal washed up on the beach.

botulism — a type of food poisoning caused by ingesting a toxin produced by the bacteria *Clostridium botulinum.*

cetacean — any of several large aquatic mammals that have forelimbs modified into flippers, a horizontally flattened tail, a nostril at the top of the head for breathing, and no hind limbs. Cetaceans include all whales, dolphins, and porpoises.

cold-blooded — having a body temperature that varies with the environment.

data — facts that can be used as a basis for calculations, reasoning, or decisions.

dehydration — loss of water from body tissues.

diagnostic — of or pertaining to the process of identifying a disease or condition on the basis of symptoms.

electrolyte — any of certain compounds that separate into electrically charged atoms or groups of atoms when mixed with water. Electrolytes are the major force in controlling fluid balance within the body.

emaciated — abnormally thin as a result of starvation or disease.

endangered — in danger of becoming extinct.

endangered species — a species of plant or animal that is in danger of becoming extinct.

endoscopy — visually examining the interior of a body cavity or hollow organ using a slender, tubular instrument.

forage — to search for and obtain food.

gastrointestinal tract — the system of organs forming the digestive pathway from the mouth to the anus, including the stomach and the intestines.

haul out — to leave the water to get on land.

hypothermia — below-normal body temperature.

Marine Mammal Protection Act (MMPA) — United States legislation that makes it illegal to hunt or harass marine mammals in U.S. waters. The primary objective of the MMPA is to maintain the health and stability of the marine ecosystem and to establish and maintain optimal sustainable populations of marine mammals.

mass stranding — the stranding of large numbers of marine mammals at the same time.

molt — to shed the exoskeleton or the outer layer of skin, hair, or feathers.

mortality — the frequency of death in a population.

parasite — on organism that lives in or on another organism, from which it gets its nourishment.

pinniped — any of several aquatic mammals characterized by having all four limbs modified into flippers. Pinnipeds include seals, sea lions, fur seals, and walruses.

pneumonia — acute inflammation of the lungs.

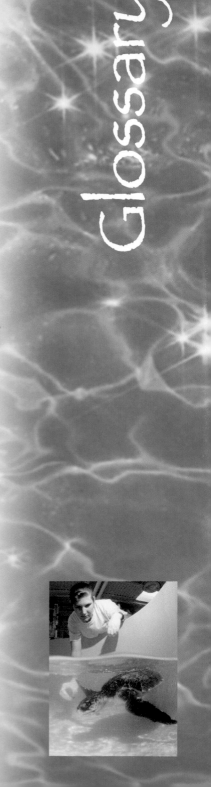

polychlorinated biphenyls (PCBs) — a group of compounds used in various industrial and agricultural processes. PCBs are a type of environmental contaminant.

rehabilitation — restoration to good health.

respiratory — of or pertaining to breathing.

satellite — a human-made device launched from the earth into orbit around a planet or the sun.

Species Survival Plan (SSP) — a program for managing the captive populations of certain threatened or endangered animals, administered by the American Zoo and Aquarium Association (AZA).

stranded animal — a live marine animal that is helpless and unable to cope in its present position. (The term is generally used to refer to marine mammals or sea turtles, but in this book it also refers to distressed birds.)

threatened species — a species of plant or animal identified as facing a possible threat of extinction, but not facing as great a threat as an endangered species. Threatened species are likely to become endangered.

toxin — a poisonous substance, especially one produced by a living organism.

transmitter — a device that sends a signal.

triage — the process of allocating medical resources and care according to degree of injury or illness, urgency of treatment, and place for treatment.

virus — any of a large group of disease-producing microbes that reproduce only in living cells.

weaned — no longer nursing from its mother; accustomed to food other than mother's milk.

Web Sites

Alliance of Marine Mammal Parks and Aquariums
www.ammpa.org

American Zoo and Aquarium Association
www.aza.org

Animal information from SeaWorld and Busch Gardens.
www.seaworld.org
www.buschgardens.org

Florida Fish and Wildlife Conservation Commission, Bureau of Protected Species Management
www.state.fl.us/gfc

Friends of the Sea Lion Marine Mammal Center
www.fslmmc.org

International Marine Animal Trainers Association
www.imata.org

National Marine Fisheries Service, Office of Protected Resources
www.nmfs.noaa.gov/prot_res/prot_res

Society for Marine Mammalogy
pegasus.cc.ucf.edu/~smm

The Marine Mammal Center
www.tmmc.org

United States Fish and Wildlife Service
www.fws.gov

Bibliography

Antrim, Jim, J.F. McBain, and Donna Parham. "Rehabilitation and Release of a Gray Whale Calf: J.J.'s Story." *Endangered Species Update* 15 (5), September–October 1998, pp. 84-89.

Byrum, Jody. *A World Beneath the Waves. Whales, Dolphins, and Porpoises.* San Diego: SeaWorld, Inc., 1998.

Byrum, Jody. *Pinnipeds From Pole to Pole. Seals, Sea Lions, and Walruses.* San Diego: SeaWorld, Inc., 2000.

Crisp, Terri and Samantha Glen. *Out of Harm's Way.* New York: Pocket Books/Simon & Schuster, Inc., 1996.

Dierauf, Leslie A., ed. *CRC Handbook of Marine Mammal Medicine: Health, Disease, and Rehabilitation.* Boca Raton, Florida: CRC Press, Inc., 1990.

DuBois, Lauren. "The Role of the Zoo in the Rehabilitation of the California Brown Pelican." *International Wildlife Rehabilitation Commission (IWRC) Conference Proceedings,* 1994, pp. 33-37.

Geraci, Joseph R. and V.J. Lounsbury. *Marine Mammals Ashore: A Field Guide for Strandings.* College Station: Texas A&M University Sea Grant College, 1993.

Goodridge, Harry and Lew Dietz. *A Seal Called Andre. The Two Worlds of a Maine Harbor Seal.* Camden, Maine: Down East Books, 1975.

Heyning, John E. and James G. Mead. "Thermoregulation in the Mouths of Gray Whales." *Science* 278, 1997, pp. 1138–1139.

Koebner, Linda. *Zoo Book. The Evolution of Wildlife Conservation Centers.* New York: Tom Doherty Associates, 1994.

Mallory, Kenneth and Andrea Conley. *Rescue of the Stranded Whales.* New York: Simon and Schuster, 1989.

McBain, Jim. "Otters and Oil Don't Mix." *Zoo Life*, Fall 1990, pp. 47-48.

Moretti, M. Mindy, ed. *Communique*. March 2000 (periodical publication of the American Zoo and Aquarium Association).

National Marine Fisheries Service. *Marine Mammal Protection Act of 1972 Annual Report*. Updated annually.

Nuzzolo, Deborah. *Dolphin Discovery. Bottlenose Dolphin Training and Interaction*. San Diego: SeaWorld, Inc., 1999.

O'Shea, Thomas J., Galen B. Rathbun, Robert K. Boncle, Claus D. Buergelt, and Daniel K. Odell, "An Epizootic of Florida Manatees Associated With a Dinoflagellate Bloom." *Marine Mammal Science 7* (2), April 1991, pp. 165-179.

Reynolds, John E. III and Sentiel A. Rommel, eds. *Biology of Marine Mammals*. Washington, D.C.: Smithsonian Institution Press, 1999.

Ridgway, Sam H., ed. *Mammals of the Sea. Biology and Medicine*. Springfield, Illinois: Charles C. Thomas, 1972.

Ridgway, Samuel. *The Dolphin Doctor*. Second edition. San Diego: Dolphin Science Press, 1995.

Twiss, John R. Jr. and Randall R. Reeves, eds. *Conservation and Management of Marine Mammals*. Washington, D.C.: Smithsonian Institution Press, 1999.

Wlodarski, Loran. *Siren's Song. The Story of Manatees*. Orlando, Florida: SeaWorld, Inc., 1998.

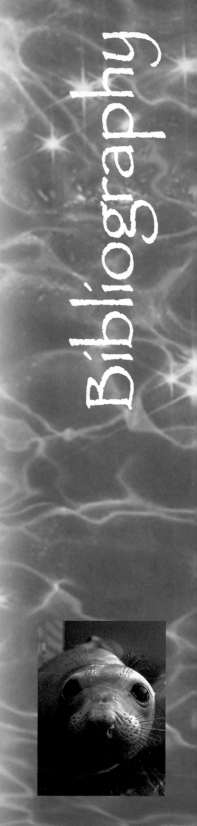

Books for Young Readers

Amato, Nicole S. and Carol A. Amato. *Raising Ursa.* Hauppauge, New York: Barron's Educational Series, 1996.

Ancona, George. *Turtle Watch.* New York: Macmillan Publishing Company, 1987.

Arnold, Caroline and Richard Hewett. *Baby Whale Rescue. The True Story of J.J.* Mahwah, New Jersey: Bridgewater Books, 1999.

Arnold, Caroline. *Sea Lion.* New York: Morrow, 1994.

Bailey, Jill. *Polar Bear Rescue.* Austin: Steck-Vaughn Company, 1992.

Carlson, Dale. *I Found A Baby Duck, What Do I Do?* Madison, Connecticut: Bick Publishing House, 1997.

Craft, Mary. *Cruz and Slick.* Pacific Grove, California: Mary Craft Publishing, 1991.

Craft, Mary. *Little Orphan Otter.* Pacific Grove, California: Mary Craft Publishing, 1989.

Darling, Kathy. *Manatee on Location.* New York: Lothrop, Lee & Shepard Books, 1991.

Dietz, Lew. *Andre.* Camden, Maine: Down East Books, 1979.

Goldner, Kathryn A. and Carole G. Vogel. *Humphrey the Wrong Way Whale.* Minneapolis, Minnesota: Dillon Press, 1987.

Hanna, Jack. *Jungle Jack Hanna's What Zoo-Keepers Do.* New York: Scholastic Inc., 1998.

Harms, John II. *The Saving of Sly Manatee.* Palm Beach Gardens, Florida: Frederick Press, 1998.

Himmelman, John. *Ibis. A True Whale Story.* New York: Scholastic, Inc., 1990.

Hodgkins, Fran. *The Orphan Seal.* Camden, Maine: Down East Books, 2000.

Jenkins, Priscilla Belz. *A Safe Home for Manatees.* New York: HarperCollins Publishers, 1997.

Kalman, Bobbie. *Sea Otters.* New York: Crabtree Publishing Company, 1997.

Kress, Stephen (as told to Pete Salmansohn). *Project Puffin: How We Brought Puffins Back to Egg Rock.* Gardiner, Maine: Tilbury House, Publishers, 1997.

Maden, Mary. *The Great Manatee Rescue.* Kill Devil Hills, North Carolina: Dog and Pony Publishing, 1999.

Meeker, Clare Hodgson. *Lootas, Little Wave Eater. An Orphaned Otter's Story.* Seattle: Sasquatch Books, 1999.

Smith, Roland. *Sea Otter Rescue.* New York: Cobblehill Books, 1990.

Tobin, Deborah. *Tangled in the Bay. The Story of a Baby Right Whale.* Halifax, Nova Scotia: Nimbus Publishing Limited, 1999.

Tokuda, Wendy and Richard Hall. *Humphrey the Lost Whale. A True Story.* Union City, California: Heian International, Inc., 1986.

Shamu TV on Video

Rescue at Sea: A Pinniped Challenge, SeaWorld, Inc., 1999.

Index

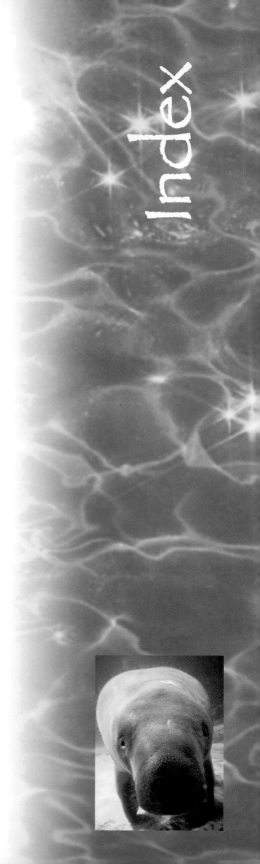

S

sea lions, 1, 4, *4*, 7, *7*, 12, 18, 20, 24, 26, 29, 43, 54, 60–61, *61*, *72–73*, *74*, 77, 81, 92, 97, *97*, *98*, *99*, *101*
California sea lion, 1, 4, 7, *7*, *13*, 18, 60, *61*, *74*, 92, *97*, *98*
See also **fur seals** *and* **seals.**
seabirds, 6, 8, 9, 13, 15, 17, 18, 43, 46, 47, 57
seals, 1, 4, 5, 6, 12, 16, *19*, 20, 24–27, *29*, *39*, 43, 54, 60–61, 75, 77, *77*, 81, *81*, 92, *95*, 97, 101, *105*
harbor seal, *39*, 60, *77*, *81*, 92
Hawaiian monk seal, 92, *95*
hooded seal, 16, 60–61
northern elephant seal, *19*, *24*, 24–27, *29*, 60, *77*, *105*
ringed seal, 60
See also **fur seals** *and* **sea lions.**
SeaWorld Cleveland, 1, 55, 56, 57, 60, 61, 70
SeaWorld Orlando, 1, 11, 16, 21, 43, 48, 49, 50, 62, 63, 66, 67, 69, 70
SeaWorld San Antonio, 1, 14, 43, 84
SeaWorld San Diego, 1, 9, 15, 24, 25, 34, 42, 43, 46, 47, 55, 60, 61, 65, 69, 70, 71, 75, 76, 78
separation from mother, 20
Species Survival Plans (SSPs), 14, 84–85, 86, 87, 102
stranded animal (definition), 4–5, 102

T

tagging, 27, 63, 77, 78–79
PIT tags, 11, 77
satellite transmitter tags, 48, *63*, *64*, 64–65, *65*, 77, *78*, 78–79, *79*, 102
Taxon Advisory Groups (TAGs), 87–88
tissue bank, *see* **National Marine Mammal Tissue Bank**
tortoises, 63
toxins, 17–18, 45, 56, 71, 93, 102
PCBs, 18, 102
brevitoxin, 17

ciguatoxin, 17
domoic acid, 18
human-made toxins, 18
tracking released animals, *25*, 77, 78–79
transporting animals, 27, 28, 29, *76*, *76*
traumatic injuries, *12*, 12–13, *13*
tube-feeding, 27, 32, *32*, 33, 34–35, *35*
turtles, 1, 5, 7, 8, 9, 13, 16, *16*, 19, 36, *36*, 43, 48, 54, *62*, 62–63, *63*, *64*, 64–65, *65*, 74, 77, *101*
green sea turtle, 62, *62*, 63, *64*, 64–65, *65*; Wrong-Way Corrigan the green sea turtle, *64*, 64–65, *65*
hawksbill sea turtle, 62
Kemp's ridley sea turtle, 16, *16*, 62, *101*
leatherback sea turtle, 62
loggerhead sea turtle, *36*, 62, *63*

U

United States Fish and Wildlife Service (USFWS), 29, 42, 43, 49, 55, 56, 59, 71, 75, 80, 85, 97

W

waterfowl, 6, 36, 57, 90–91
walruses, 4, 12, 43, 54, 60, *60*, 101
whale lice, *6*, 7
whales, 1, 4, 5, 7, 8, 13, 21, 29, 43, 54, 66–67, *67*, 75, 76, *76*, 77, 81, 100
beluga whale, 13
Bryde's whale, 66, *67*
dwarf sperm whale, 67
false killer whale, 67
gray whale, 8, *8*, 34–35, *35*, 38, 66, *76*, *76*, 96, *96*; J.J. the gray whale, 34–35, *35*, 38, 66, *76*, *76*, 96, *96*
killer whale, 12, *50*, 67
pilot whale, 67
pygmy killer whale, 67
pygmy sperm whale, *32*, 66, *66*
sperm whale, 67
See also **dolphins.**
watercraft, 12, 13, 62–63, 68–69